Kitchen & Bath

PROJECT COSTS

RSMeans

Kitchen&Bath

PROJECT COSTS

*Planning
& Estimating
Successful
Projects*

 Reed Construction Data.

Copyright © 2005
Reed Construction Data, Inc.
Construction Publishers & Consultants
63 Smiths Lane
Kingston, MA 02364-0800
781-422-5000
www.rsmeans.com
RSMeans is a product line of Reed Construction Data

Managing Editor: Mary Greene. Editors: Andrea Sillah and Robert W. Mewis, CCC. Editorial Assistant: Jessica Deady. Production Manager: Michael Kokernak. Composition: Jonathan Forgit. Proofreaders: Alice McSharry and Robin Richardson. Book and cover design: Norman R. Forgit. Contributing Photographer: Norm Forgit. Illustrations: Christina Trager. Cover photographs are copyright Peter Vanderwarker and Nancy Fenton.

Printed in the United States of America

10 9 8 7 6 5 4 3 2 1

Library of Congress Catalog Number Pending

ISBN 0-87629-784-X

Table of Contents

Acknowledgments

The editors thank Peter Vanderwarker, of Peter Vanderwarker Photographs in West Newton, MA, for allowing us to reprint the bath photograph featured on the cover. The room was designed by architect Diana Bailey. FENTON Inc. was the general contractor.

Special thanks to Nancy Fenton for use of her kitchen photograph, also on the cover. This space was designed by C & J Katz Studio. Again, FENTON Inc. was the general contractor.

We would also like to acknowledge the National Kitchen and Bath Association (NKBA) for granting permission to reprint several illustrations from their kitchen and bathroom planning guidelines, and Travis Industries for allowing us to use a photograph of their Bed and Breakfast™ gas fireplace.

Howard Chandler, Executive Officer of the Builders Association of Greater Boston, a chapter of the National Association of Home Builders (NAHB), reviewed and offered helpful input on several sections of the book.

And finally, our appreciation to the Remodelors Council of the National Association of Home Builders, who provided guidelines for the section titled, "A Few Thoughts on Marketing."

Introduction

Kitchen and bath projects are a source of big profits for remodeling contractors. There's a huge demand for this work, as homeowners look for ways to increase the quality of their lives and the value of their homes. They're often willing to invest more in these types of improvements because of the proven return in resale value.

These projects can also be complex in a number of ways. A variety of different items typically have to be ordered, delivered, and scheduled carefully for installation in the right sequence and within a strict time frame. Kitchen and bath renovations can vary in scope from all-encompassing—design and complete installation—to only certain elements. This will depend on the homeowner's approach, whether they're consulting with a designer, and whether they're contracting specialty installers directly.

How This Book Can Help You

The Project Estimates

The bulk of this book consists of sample kitchen and bath projects with estimates. The model projects range from simple jobs like replacing a fixture or countertop to complete renovations of different kitchen and bath layouts. The "model" for each project estimate is based on a typical floor plan, using fixtures and materials available at most home centers. Each estimate includes:

- All the materials that would be needed for the project, with unit and total costs
- Labor-hours to install (and demolish and remove) each item
- Subcontractor costs for certain trades and services
- An allocation for overhead and profit
- Total contractor cost

Plus "Alternates"—unit costs for different finishes and fixtures so you can adjust the estimate to your project's particular features.

Use these estimates as checklists to make sure:

- You've included everything if you're planning a similar job.
- Your own bid estimate is in the right range for typical contractor costs.

The project estimate costs can be adjusted to pricing conditions in your specific area using the "Location Factors" in the back of the book. These easy-to-apply factors are given for more than 900 individual areas in the U.S. and Canada, organized by zip code.

Project Tips

Each of the model projects also includes tips on what to consider when planning these installations and selecting fixtures.

Also check out the introductions to the "Kitchens" and "Baths" sections. Each has helpful information on available fixtures and materials, unit cost ranges, standard clearances, and design and layout recommendations.

Estimating & Business Guidance

Part One offers some advice on things that remodeling contractors need to know and do well to be successful. There's no question that you need to accurately estimate project costs in order to be competitive, while making a worthwhile profit. So the first section, immediately following this introduction, reviews the different **types of estimates and steps in the process**, including the all-important site visit and evaluation of existing conditions.

Among the points covered is allocating the right amount of time and effort to estimating, based on the type and purpose of the estimate. For example, rough "ballpark" estimates, for preliminary discussion with homeowners, can be quick, off-the-cuff figures based on similar projects or the project total costs given in this book.

Detailed estimates, on the other hand, needed for bidding a job, require a careful, thorough site visit and evaluation, and systematic takeoff and pricing. Unit price, or bid, estimates are based on actual wage rates and subcontractor and material costs, and your own records of labor-hours based on similar, recent projects.

The estimating section ends with takeoff and pricing forms. You can either photocopy them from the book, or access and print them from the book's Web site: **http://www.rsmeans.com/ supplement/67347.asp.**

Next is a discussion about **contracts** between you and the homeowner, and some items that should be included in these documents. After that, you'll find **tips for working with homeowners** to help make the project go as smoothly as possible, resulting in a more pleasant experience for everyone—and great references at the end of the job. The next sections list some points to consider when **remodeling older and antique homes** and incorporating **"green building"** materials. The last of the front sections include **"A Few Thoughts on Marketing"** and **"Closing the Sale,"** and include insights from the National Association of Home Builders' Remodelors Council.

Along with the **"Location Factors,"** the back of the book includes **"Safety Tips"** and **"Resources"**—a list of Web sites and other contact information for manufacturers, professional associations, and other helpful sources.

The Rewards

Even with all the challenges, kitchen and bath remodeling is a great specialty. It's steady and profitable work, and you're filling a real demand in your community. As you gain experience and a sense of how long the work will take, what the potential complications are, and how much various features will cost, you can develop an excellent business with a kitchen and bath focus.

Part One

Planning & Estimating the Project

Estimating Project Costs

Estimating is one of the most important aspects of the job. Its purpose is to calculate as accurately as possible the anticipated costs of labor, materials, and equipment; overhead costs; and a reasonable profit. Errors in calculations or failure to fully review the plans and specifications (when provided) or to understand the scope of work can be costly. Reliable estimates are essential to your success.

Assembling an estimate can take hours of hard work with no assurance that you'll get the job... but it's also an opportunity to gain profitable work. Larger-volume contractors may bid as many as ten jobs in order to win just one. Their success often depends on having an organized system in place so they can prepare estimates efficiently and accurately.

Different Estimates for Different Purposes

Ballpark Estimates

Contractors are called on to develop estimates for different situations. Homeowners, especially those you've worked for on other jobs, might ask you to provide a rough cost so they can see if a project is in the realm of possibility for them financially. This "ballpark" price will probably be based on your past experience with similar projects, allowing for differences in project size or complications. The project estimates in this book or costs from other RSMeans publications* can also help you generate quick, rough estimates.

Detailed Estimates

When it comes time to provide your client with a written bid for an actual job, you'll need to create a detailed "unit price" estimate of labor, material, equipment, and overhead and profit—based on plans, specifications, a schedule, material and labor costs, and subcontractor quotes. Every estimate requires that you specifically define the quantity—and quality—of materials to be installed.

Units of measure for estimating must also be defined, such as square feet of drywall or flooring, linear feet of molding, or "each" in the case of a stand-alone item like a sink, appliance, or light fixture. Next, the units are counted, and then they're priced.

Labor calculations require consideration not only of how long the work will take, hourly rate, and benefits, but factors like a particular worker or crew's productivity, use of unfamiliar equipment, and access issues at the site that make the work go more slowly. Bids from subcontractors should be reviewed to make sure they include all work and materials.

The main estimate references for a project are plans created by an architect or designer (if available), subcontractor quotes, your own experience, and details that you have noted based on a careful inspection of site conditions and the client's specifications. If you have questions about plans prepared by an architect or designer, get them answered at the start.

Scope of Work

To understand the scope of work, you need to identify construction methods, site conditions, and quality (including manufacturer and model numbers) and quantity of materials, fixtures, and finishes. You also need to clarify which, if any, materials or fixtures the homeowner will provide, and other items that have a cost, including insurance, permits, architect or engineer's stamp, storage, or special equipment.

Existing Site Conditions & the Site Visit

In new construction, the contractor usually relies on building plans and some type of specifications as the major reference when preparing an estimate. Remodeling projects, on the other hand, are heavily dependent on site conditions, some of which may not be known until the work is under way.

Remodeling contractors need to carefully evaluate existing conditions, in as much detail as possible, to determine how these factors will affect the cost of the planned renovation. If there are concealed conditions that cannot be known until the work is in progress, the estimate should include a contingency, or the contract should provide for coverage of such expenses.

* Means *Contractor Pricing Guides* and *Home Improvement Cost Guides* are all available at home centers and bookstores.

Even if you have detailed plans for your project, you still need to anticipate any conditions that will:

- Restrict your work—such as working in a cramped space, or having to leave appliances in place for the homeowner's use during a kitchen remodel, and working around them.

- Complicate and add to the work— such as the need to replace structural members and underlayment due to water damage hidden under the flooring, or removing and replacing a window in order to get a large item into the space.

During the site visit, you need to envision the work to be done on the project, including items that may not be directly specified or obvious. Try to anticipate material handling problems and measure clearances for items that can't be broken down, like a whirlpool tub or a large L-shaped countertop. This will help reduce the chance of unexpected costs and change orders.

Subcontractors should also visit the site to help identify complications and to clarify their part of the job. This is a good time to clear up which trade will be responsible for things like providing wood backing for bathroom fixtures, or cutting and patching holes for wiring. Subcontractors' familiarity with building code requirements also helps you identify any additional structural, electrical, or plumbing work that may have to be done along with the renovation.

From the Bottom Up

Usually the best way to evaluate an existing structure is from the bottom up. This enables you to see how the structure was built and to trace the plumbing, heating, and electrical systems from below. Sometimes problems like structural weakness or moisture intrusion need to be dealt with in order to prepare for remodeling. Consult an architect or engineer on questions of structural integrity.

Dimensions & Variations in Construction Standards

Every house is different, and your work has to be built around the existing conditions. Ceiling heights in older homes may vary from one part of the house to another and may be irregular because of settling. If a floor is extremely out of level, each stud in a new partition wall may have to be cut to a different length.

Be sure to record dimensions to help you plan material quantities and the work involved. Also, note dimensions of doorways, hallways, and stairways that will be your access route when bringing in potentially large materials and equipment for the job.

Plumbing & HVAC

The condition of existing piping can have a big effect on new fixture installations. Corrosion or pitting of exposed piping may indicate similar conditions where it's concealed in walls or ceilings. It's a good idea to check,

where possible, the inside of pipes for scaling. Old galvanized pipes may be encrusted and restricting water flow. This problem should be addressed before new work begins.

Gaskets, seals, and shut-off valves should also be checked for general condition and function. If existing fixtures are to be replaced, rough-in dimensions should be measured to make sure they match the new fixtures. New rough-ins may require jogs and extra fittings, with more labor involved. Walls and ceilings may have to be cut and patched.

If the project involves moving fixtures to a different wall, pipes, drains, and vents may all have to be moved. During the site visit, pipes might be located by looking beneath the floor if it's accessible. You can also check in the attic and on the roof for vent pipes. In some cases, they're offset, and not directly over the pipes in the kitchen or bathroom walls.

Ductwork for ventilation systems should be carefully planned to make sure there is adequate space. You'll also want to identify possible conflicts between the ductwork, piping, electrical, and structural elements.

Electrical

During the site visit, you should also note the home's electrical capacity and location of outlets for equipment you need to perform the work.

Your electrical subcontractor should be knowledgeable in both national and local electrical codes. To avoid conflicts between national and local codes, as well as complications with the building inspector after the work is completed, you may want to include in your contract a phrase similar to the following:

"Perform all electrical work in compliance with applicable codes and ordinances, even when in conflict with the drawings and specifications." Any code questions or conflicts should be raised and resolved as early as possible.

Some codes now require that major appliances in the kitchen have their own circuits. (This would also apply to sauna or steam units that might be included in a spa-style bathroom.) Consult your local building authority to clarify these requirements.

If the project requires an upgrade in electrical service, the cost needs to be identified. If existing walls and ceilings are to remain in place, access holes must be made in order to snake wiring, and then the holes must be patched.

More on Cutting & Patching

Almost every remodeling job involves a good deal of cutting, patching, and repainting to match the surrounding conditions. Access holes must be opened in walls or between floors to install wire, conduit, and/or piping. If the walls or floors are fire-rated, fire-stopping caulk and sealant may be needed to seal penetrations.

For some projects, it's more cost-effective to remove and re-install new walls and ceilings (as done in the whole-room remodel project estimates in this book), rather than cutting and patching. Not only do you get access to wiring and piping, but the new walls will be plumb and square, making tasks like cabinet installation go more smoothly.

For a partial room remodel, the original moldings and trim must be carefully removed and replaced. Any damaged pieces will have to be re-created or repaired, which takes time and expense. If access holes have to be cut in a wallpapered or tiled wall, you may not be able to match the original materials to make a seamless repair. In these cases, a whole wall or room may need new finishes.

A careful site visit and inspection will often reveal unusual materials or potential complications so that you can account for their cost. For example, if a new plumbing vent has to penetrate a slate shingle roof, the requirements might include a custom-made copper sleeve and flashing, replacement of broken shingles, and even scaffolding to access the roof without damaging it. The cost would be many times what it would be for the same work on an asphalt shingle roof.

Other Items to Check

Find out where materials can be stored and if there are any restrictions on the hours during which power equipment can be used. Determine whether there will be complications in the demolition part of the project, including the presence of hazards such as lead paint or asbestos pipe coverings. Take note of any access restrictions inside and out,

and whether there is available space for storing materials and for a dumpster or portable toilet, if needed for the job.

Demolition & Dumpster Rental

A thorough site visit includes specifically identifying and noting materials to be demolished or removed, since the costs can differ substantially from one material to another. (For example, removing gypsum plaster on metal lath is about three times more costly than nailed drywall.) Demolition involves dismantling and removing existing materials, appliances, and fixtures; transporting them to a dumpster or truck; and hauling them to an approved dump.

To estimate demolition, contractors usually rely on experience with similar jobs, a schedule for the work, and knowledge of dump and dumpster restrictions and fees. If asbestos or other hazardous materials need to be removed, consult local authorities and a licensed subcontractor. Not only is there a health hazard, but EPA and OSHA impose stiff fines and penalties when hazardous materials are handled and discarded improperly.

Protecting Adjacent Spaces & Finished Work

During the site visit, you should also note the layout of the house and the specific requirements for protecting adjacent spaces from damage and dust during the project. Labor and materials to protect against dust, debris, and foot traffic are necessary cost items.

Creating the Estimate

The following items need to be addressed in a thorough estimate:

- Quantity and quality of materials and equipment
- Existing conditions at the project site
- Availability of workers and subcontractors, their productivity, their rates, and the quality of their work
- How long the job will take and how tight the schedule is
- Effects of the weather or season, such as cold and damp, or hot and dry conditions that may affect the schedule for finishing flooring, painting, plastering, and other tasks
- Overhead directly related to this job
- The amount of your overall company overhead (including vehicles, tools, and equipment; marketing; and bookkeeping and other office expenses) that will be applied to this job

The estimate steps include:

- Quantity takeoff
- Pricing each item and multiplying by the number of items
- Including subcontractor quotes after you've reviewed them to make sure they include all tasks and materials
- Adding a contingency, if necessary, and overhead and profit
- Putting the estimate in the appropriate format for bidding

Overhead & Profit

Be sure your final estimate includes not only the "hard" costs (material and labor), but the right amount for "soft" costs, such as overhead, profit, insurance, and temporary items (such as dumpster, portable toilet, or scaffolding rental).

The amount to include for profit is a decision many contractors make on a case-by-case basis. For example, you might be willing to accept less profit in order to win a particular job that will boost your reputation or chances for future work. On the other hand, you might choose to increase the profit for a high-risk job that will require more time to manage.

Organizing the Estimate

Using forms, whether paper or on the computer, is a helpful way to organize estimates and make sure you've included everything. Forms can be organized in different ways. For a large, complicated project, you might want to use a form to list, quantify, and price the items in each major category of work, such as carpentry, plumbing, painting, etc.— then summarize the totals on a summary estimate sheet.

The following pages are takeoff and pricing forms that list a broad range of items you may need for kitchen and bath projects. Each has columns for quantifying and pricing the items, and for noting the source (vendor), model numbers, and any specifications. There is also a form for purchase or rental of tools and equipment. These forms are also available on the book's Web site to print or customize: **http://www.rsmeans.com/supplement/67347.asp.**

Kitchen Remodeling Takeoff Form

	Unit	Quantity	Price per Unit	Total	Dimensions	Source/Model #/ Specs
Walls						
Gypsum board						
gypsum board, 3/8"						
gypsum board, 1/2"						
gypsum board, water-resistant, 1/2"						
cement board						
joint compound						
wallboard accessories						
plaster and accessories						
Framing lumber						
1 x 4						
2 x 3						
2 x 4						
2 x 6						
2 x 8						
2 x 10						
2 x 12						
4 x 4						
Plywood						
AC birch, 1/4"						
AC birch, 3/4"						
hardboard underlay, 3/16"						
underlayment, 5/8"						
interior, 1/2"						
CDX, 5/8"						
Insulation						
fiberglass batt, kraft-faced, 3-1/2"						
fiberglass batt, kraft-faced, 6"						

	Unit	Quantity	Price per Unit	Total	Dimensions	Source/Model #/ Specs
Insulation (cont.)						
fiberglass batt, foil-faced, 6"						
fiberglass batt, unfaced, 6"						
rigid molded beadboard, 1/2"						
Vapor barrier						
Molding						
baseboard, pine						
crown molding						
1 x 3						
door casing						
window casing						
Paint						
paint						
stain						
urethane						
drop cloth						
brushes						
sandpaper						
Wall covering						
wallpaper						
vinyl wall covering						
wallpaper paste/adhesive						
Wall tile						
ceramic/stone						
glass						
metal						

	Unit	Quantity	Price per Unit	Total	Dimensions	Source/Model #/ Specs
Wall tile (cont.)						
grout						
cement and sealer						
Shelving						
wood						
plastic laminate-covered wood						
Flooring						
Wood flooring						
unfinished wood						
prefinished wood						
wood laminate						
Tile flooring						
quarry tile						
ceramic tile						
stone tile						
tile base						
grout						
adhesive						
sealer						
Resilient flooring						
sheet vinyl						
vinyl tile						
laminate						
baseboard trim						
cement						
floor filler						

	Unit	Quantity	Price per Unit	Total	Dimensions	Source/Model #/ Specs
Linoleum flooring						
plywood underlayment						
underlayment transition thresholds						
cementitious backerboard						
nails — flooring and finishing						
baseboard trim						
cement						
floor filler						
Cabinets						
base						
wall						
island						
corner						
pantry						
bookcase						
appliance garage(s)						
lazy susan(s)						
pull-out shelves or trash bins						
other interior special features						
valance, cornice trim						
blocking						
mounting screws						
Cabinet Re-Facing						
Cabinet doors						
wood						
laminate over composite						
glass						

	Unit	Quantity	Price per Unit	Total	Dimensions	Source/Model #/ Specs
drawer fronts						
laminate facing material						
Countertops						
plastic laminate						
solid surface						
ceramic tile						
granite or other stone						
butcher block						
plywood base, 3/4"						
support framing/corbels						
adhesive						
trim						
edging						
Light Fixtures & Other Electrical						
Lights						
undercabinet						
in-cabinet						
pendant						
recessed						
track strip and fixtures						
chandelier						
wall washers						
wall sconces						
Vents and fans						
soffit vent						
rafter vent						
ceiling fan						

	Unit	Quantity	Price per Unit	Total	Dimensions	Source/Model #/ Specs
Vents and fans (cont.)						
vent exhaust fan						
fan/light ceiling fixture						
Switches						
light switches						
dimmer switches						
accessible switches						
Receptacles						
common						
GFI						
telephone						
internet						
cable						
Boxes						
Wire						
Coaxial						
power						
sound						
twisted pair						
Speakers						
Baseboard heat						

	Unit	Quantity	Price per Unit	Total	Dimensions	Source/Model #/ Specs
Appliances						
range						
range hood						
cooktop						
microwave						
convection oven						
refrigerator(s)						
dishwasher(s)						
wine refrigerator						
wall oven(s) (regular and warming)						
disposal						
trash compactor						
Plumbing						
Main sink						
stainless						
enameled steel						
stone						
solid surface						
porcelain						
Second (e.g., island) sink						
stainless						
enameled steel						
stone						
solid surface						
porcelain						
Laundry sink						

	Unit	Quantity	Price per Unit	Total	Dimensions	Source/Model #/ Specs
Pot filler						
Faucets/fittings						
Faucet attachments/accessories						
soap dispenser						
sprayer						
water-filtration system						
accessible levers/handles						
Instant hot water dispenser						
Ice-maker						
Traps						
Drain Ts, elbows, caps, pipe						
Supply Ts, elbows, caps, pipe						
Copper tubing, 3/8"						
PVC piping						
PVC cement						
Solder						

	Unit	Quantity	Price per Unit	Total	Dimensions	Source/Model #/ Specs
Fireplaces, Gas or Wood-Burning						
face						
chimney						
vent						
piping						
Doors & Windows						
Flush interior door						
6-panel interior door						
Hollow-core, pre-hung interior door						
French doors, interior or exterior						
Pocket door						
Bi-fold closet door						
By-pass closet door						
Casement window						
Half-round window						
Skylights						
fixed						
operable						

	Unit	Quantity	Price per Unit	Total	Dimensions	Source/Model #/ Specs
Hardware & Fasteners						
Nails						
Screws						
Hinges						
Drawer and cabinet pulls						
Passage set door knob, no lock						
Accessible pulls						

Bathroom Remodeling Takeoff Form

	Unit	Quantity	Price per Unit	Total	Dimensions	Source/Model #/Specs
Walls						
Gypsum board						
gypsum board, 3/8"						
gypsum board, 1/2"						
gypsum board, water-resistant, 1/2"						
cement board						
joint compound						
wallboard accessories						
Plaster and accessories						
Framing lumber						
1 x 4						
2 x 3						
2 x 4						
2 x 6						
2 x 8						
2 x 10						
2 x 12						
4 x 4						
Plywood						
AC birch, 1/4"						
AC birch, 3/4"						
hardboard underlay, 3/16"						
underlayment, 5/8"						
interior, 1/2"						
CDX, 5/8"						
Insulation						
fiberglass batt, kraft-faced, 3-1/2"						

	Unit	Quantity	Price per Unit	Total	Dimensions	Source/Model #/ Specs
Insulation (cont.)						
fiberglass batt, kraft-faced, 6"						
fiberglass batt, foil-faced, 6"						
fiberglass batt, unfaced, 6"						
rigid molded beadboard, 1/2"						
sound-proofing insulation						
Polyethylene vapor barrier						
Molding						
baseboard, pine						
crown molding						
1 x 3						
door casing						
window casing						
Paint						
paint						
stain						
urethane						
drop cloth						
brushes						
sandpaper						
Wallcovering						
wallpaper						
vinyl wallcovering						
wallpaper paste/adhesive						

	Unit	Quantity	Price per Unit	Total	Dimensions	Source/Model #/ Specs
Wall tile						
ceramic/stone						
glass						
metal						
grout						
Shelving						
wood						
plastic laminate-covered						
Flooring						
Tile flooring						
ceramic tile						
stone tile						
tile base						
grout						
adhesive						
sealer						
Resilient flooring						
sheet vinyl						
vinyl tile						
laminate						
Plywood 1/2" underlayment						
Nails – flooring and finishing						
Baseboard trim						

	Unit	Quantity	Price per Unit	Total	Dimensions	Source/Model #/ Specs
Furniture & Accessories						
Vanity cabinets						
wood						
laminate over wood composite						
Mirror						
Towel bar(s) or rings						
Toilet tissue dispenser						
Robe hook(s)						
Shower curtain rod						
Grab bars						
Shower seat						
Cabinets						
Vanity Countertop						
Plastic laminate						
Solid surface						
Ceramic tile						
Stone						
Cultured stone						

	Unit	Quantity	Price per Unit	Total	Dimensions	Source/Model #/ Specs
Plywood base, 3/4"						
Adhesive						
Trim						
Light Fixtures & Other Electrical						
Fixtures						
light bar						
vanity light						
pendant light						
recessed light						
track light strip and fixtures						
chandelier						
wall sconces						
vapor-proof down lights						
Vents and fans						
vent exhaust fan and ductwork						
vent/heat/light ceiling fixture						
paddle fan						
Switches						
light switch						
dimmer switch						
whirlpool switch						
fan switch						
Receptacles						
common						
GFI						

	Unit	Quantity	Price per Unit	Total	Dimensions	Source/Model #/ Specs
Boxes						
Wire						
Coaxial						
power						
sound						
twisted pair						
Heat						
baseboard						
convection heater						
heater with fan for base of vanity						
toe-kick space heater						
under-floor radiant heating						
Plumbing						
Fixtures						
toilet						
two-piece						
one-piece						
elongated						
pressure-assisted						
vacuum flush						
bathtub						
acrylic						
metal						
fiberglass						

	Unit	Quantity	Price per Unit	Total	Dimensions	Source/Model #/ Specs
whirlpool tub						
acrylic						
fiberglass						
shower stall						
acrylic						
fiberglass						
solid surface						
stone tile						
shower pan						
lavatory						
china						
porcelain						
metal						
stone						
solid surface, integrated						
Fittings (including faucets/controls)						
lavatory						
shower						
tub						
whirlpool						
toilet						
bidet						
Special plumbing						
anti-scald device						
re-circulating hot water system						

	Unit	Quantity	Price per Unit	Total	Dimensions	Source/Model #/ Specs
Accessories and piping						
traps						
drain Ts, elbows, caps, pipe						
supply Ts, elbows, caps, pipe						
copper tubing, 37/8"						
PVC piping						
PVC cement						
solder						
valves						
Doors, Windows, & Partitions						
Flush interior door						
6-panel interior door						
Hollow-core, pre-hung interior door						
Bi-fold closet door						
By-pass closet door						
Pocket door						
Shower door						
Hardware & Fasteners						
Nails						
Screws						

	Unit	Quantity	Price per Unit	Total	Dimensions	Source/Model #/ Specs
Hinges						
Drawer and cabinet pulls						
Passage set						
Privacy set door knob with privacy lock						
Closet system						
Pedestal sink wall bracket						
Lever handles						

	Unit	Quantity	Price per Unit	Total	Dimensions	Source/Model #/ Specs

Tools & Equipment to Rent or Purchase

	Model	Purchase Price	Daily Rental Cost	Number of Days Rented
Flooring				
floor edgers				
floor staplers				
hardwood floor nailers				
Pergo® installation kits				
tile cutters				
tile rollers				
tile saws				
tile strippers				
vinyl tile stripper				
Framing				
breakers				
brute breakers				
demolition hammers				
drills				
finish nailers				
low-velocity powder-actuated fasteners				
pneumatic framing nailers				
screwguns				
underlay spot nailers				
vibratory plate compactors				
Ladders				
extension ladders				
stepladders				
Painting/Wallcovering				
airless paint sprayers				
heat gun blowers				
mud/mixing paddles				

	Model	Purchase Price	Daily Rental Cost	Number of Days Rented
Painting/Wallcovering (cont.)				
piston sprayers/carts				
texture sprayers with compressors				
wallpaper steamers				
Plumbing				
basin wrenches				
centrifugal pumps				
chain wrenches				
conduit and pipe cutters				
drain cleaners				
E.M.T. benders				
pipe reamers				
pipe stands				
pipe threaders				
pipe wrenches				
roofer's pumps				
sail pipe cutters				
sewer snakes				
toilet augers				
welders				
Sanding				
belt sanders				
drywall sanders				
floor sanders				
grinders/mini grinders				
orbit sanders				
palm sanders				
vibrator sander				

	Model	Purchase Price	Daily Rental Cost	Number of Days Rented
Saws				
band saws				
chop saws				
circular saws				
compound miter saws				
jamb saws				
jigsaws				
reciprocating saws				
table saws				
tile saws and stands				
Other Equipment				
bolt cutters				
dollies				
dumpster				
extension cords				
fans				
fishtape				
floodlights				
generator				
insulation blowers				
laser levels				
routers				
wet/dry vacuum				

	Model	Purchase Price	Daily Rental Cost	Number of Days Rented

The Contract

Both you and your customer benefit from a detailed written agreement. This agreement, or contract, sets forth in a legally binding manner the expectations that you and the owner have of one another. For you, the contract has two main purposes: it's a tool to help you manage the project, and it protects your financial interests.

Even the most basic contract should specify what's being built, and when. It should also describe the anticipated quality and cost of the work, how and when payments will be made, how changes and disputes will be handled, and how long (and to what extent) the work is guaranteed.

Types of Contracts

Different types of contractual arrangements may be used based on the situation and the risks. **Lump sum contracts** specify a payment amount based on a defined scope of work. You'll need to state in the contract that if the owner wants to add to or change the work, he or she will be responsible for related costs. Owners often prefer this arrangement because they know the total price up-front. You have the risk of estimating the work correctly, so that it can be completed on time, for the price you specified. Progress payments may be made when certain established percentages of the work are complete.

A **cost plus fee contract** is sometimes used in order to get a project going before all the details of the work are known. It involves an agreement on the general scope of work, and that you will be reimbursed for your actual costs plus a negotiated flat fee. This method

requires that you set a reasonable fee that includes profit, and keep accurate and detailed records of your actual costs, so you can justify your expenses. Sometimes this type of contract has a "not-to-exceed" price.

A **labor only contract** pays you for just that, hours worked. This type of contract may be used if the owner furnishes all the materials. The advantage is not having to purchase materials, but the drawbacks include the possibility of incorrect materials, inferior quality of materials, inadequate quantities, or having to wait for the owner to obtain additional items.

What Contracts Include

Most contracts address the following items. You might modify yours to address special payment or other considerations.

- Your company name, address, telephone and fax numbers, and license number.

- The owner's name, address, and telephone number (including cell or pager numbers).

- Scope of Work: A description of the work you will perform. If plans have been provided by an architect or kitchen/bath designer, they are part of the scope of work. You might want to include a statement in the contract that in the event the plans do not reflect building code requirements, the work will be done in compliance with the code. (You'll need to bring any such conflicts to the owner's attention as soon as they're discovered.)

- Specifications: A detailed list of the products and materials that you or your subcontractors will install. (Include manufacturer, model number, colors, dimensions, and any other important information for each product.)

- Warranties: covering materials, products, and workmanship. Include time limits and full versus limited warranty.

- Schedule: The planned schedule for the project, including the estimated start and finish dates, and any major milestone dates, such as completion of percentages of the work, to go along with partial payments. In addition to progress payments, the schedule may include other deadlines for the owner, such as product decisions and delivery of materials/products they plan to provide.

- Responsibilities: What you will be responsible for, in addition to the construction, including obtaining permits and inspections, cleanup (daily, weekly, final), dumpster and removal of rubbish, etc.

- Price: This will be the total price for the entire job, for a lump sum (or fixed-price) contract.

- Pay Schedule: Completion dates for portions of the work and expected payment. For example, a payment may be due when 50% of the work is complete, and the another payment when it's 100% complete.

- Conditions of the Contract:
  - Change Orders: Method for dealing with any changes the owner requests once the work has started. A statement that changes require

written authorization from the owner, and that the resulting extra expenses are the owner's responsibility. (It's important to get your client's commitment to final approval and clarification of all work, products, and materials at the start. Make sure they understand that delays and additional costs can result from changes.)

– Delays in the Schedule: A statement that expected start and completion dates are approximate and may be affected by unforeseen conditions such as weather, material and equipment delays, and changes to the work, and that in these cases, the schedule will be adjusted accordingly.

– Method for Dispute Resolution: An arbitration clause in the contract that directs you and your client to resolve a dispute, if one should arise, by mediation before any litigation.

– Hidden Conditions: A clause stating that you're not responsible for extra costs resulting from hidden existing conditions discovered during the work. Such conditions should be brought to the owner's attention as soon as they're discovered. It should also be stated that if hazardous materials are discovered, this agreement does not cover the cost of their removal or remediation.

– Safety: A statement that you will make every effort to keep the work site safe, and that you're not responsible for injuries incurred by others on the site.

– Scope of Agreement: A statement that this contract reflects the entire agreement between you and the owner, and takes precedence over any and all previous written or oral agreements.

• Your signature, with company name and date signed.

• The owner's signature, with date signed.

Some owners may request these additional provisions in the agreement:

• Certificate of insurance, showing that you're properly covered, with your insurance company named.

• Right of Recision clause that allows them to withdraw from the agreement within 72 hours of signing.

• Release of Liens statement that protects them in the event of debts you have incurred.

The Contract as a Management Tool

The goal of the project is to meet the requirements of the contract. Good, solid contract documents that convey a mutual understanding and commitment to perform are the ingredients of a successful project, a satisfied customer, and a successful career. Mutual understanding is the most important point for builders and remodelers. All issues should be agreed on and understood by both parties.

Changes can happen quickly when the work is in progress. Decisions made "on the fly" that don't seem important at the time can turn into major disputes at the end of the project when bills are being submitted. Many builders lose money in order to avoid dragging out a conflict. As the builder, however, you're the construction professional leading the project, and as the leader, customers expect you to explain the contract and keep records of changes and decisions.

Maintenance & Warranty Information

Often, problems occur after the project is completed because the owner fails to properly care for the new space and the items in it. Even though the problems may not have anything to do with the initial construction, the customer may expect you to fix them. One way to avoid this situation is to provide the owner with written maintenance instructions when you complete the job. These can be given along with warranty information on the products you have installed.

Organizations such as the National Association of Home Builders offer pre-printed booklets with maintenance guidelines for homeowners. *(See the "Resources" at the back of this book for contact information.)*

Note: This text is intended to offer basic guidelines on contracts. We recommend consulting an attorney on legal matters, including lien laws. Much of the information in this section is based on guidance offered in Best Business Practices for Builders & Remodelers: An Easy-to-Use Checklist System. *This book provides a quick and easy checklist system that will help you upgrade all aspects of your business, also published by RSMeans.*

Working with Homeowners

The Early Planning Stage

A kitchen or bath remodeling project can be exciting, but also stressful for homeowners. In the early planning stage, they'll have major decisions to make, and will need to carefully consider financial issues such as how much they can spend, how much their investment might return when they sell their house, and their overall wants and needs for the new space. They'll need to define the project in terms of features that are important to them now and over the next few years. If you're the homeowner's primary advisor on design, you'll want to start with their goals for the space and a rough budget. Are they interested in:

• Updating/changing the room's appearance?

• Improving the layout?

• Opening the space up – either visually or in terms of adding more square footage?

• Upgrading with higher-quality new fixtures, cabinets, countertops, flooring, appliances, and lighting?

How much of what they want can realistically be covered by their budget? By helping define the rough scope of the project, you can determine what their budget will buy. Then you can move on to design and selection of materials and products.

The Design Stage

When it comes to design, homeowners will have seemingly endless decisions to make, from the layout of their kitchen or bath to the quality, style, and finish of their new cabinets or fixtures, to the color of the walls and tile grout. If they choose to get professional design help, they'll have to go through the process of selecting and working with an architect, interior designer, Certified Kitchen or Bath Designer, or home center sales person to help them translate their ideas into actual products and a working plan.

Of course, many builders with design knowledge and experience also work directly with homeowners on layout, product decisions, and drawing up plans, especially when there are no structural changes or the need for an architect's stamp on the plans. Home centers and kitchen and bath specialty shops often help out by including a design plan as part of their services. Many manufacturers also provide design guidelines and suggested layouts that use their products.

Interviewing with the Client

When homeowners get to the point of interviewing contractors, they'll need to find ways to evaluate each candidate's skills and reliability. When you meet with a potential customer at their home, bring your licensing and insurance information, a list of several references with contact information, and some quality photos of your work. If you belong to any professional associations, let customers know. Try to anticipate the information they'll be looking for, and be ready to provide it in an organized way. Good customer service begins at this stage.

Ask to see the plans if an architect or designer has drawn them up for the project, or any sketches the owner has made. Bring up any initial questions and take notes. Look over the area that will be involved in the renovation, and mention (and write down) any major issues. If and when you take the next step to bid the job, you'll want to visit the site again and evaluate the conditions in detail before preparing your estimate. (*See "Estimating Project Costs" earlier in Part One.*)

Let the homeowner know if you specialize in the type of work they're interested in and how much experience you have with similar projects. Discuss the schedule and how soon you could start work, which parts of the work you'll be subcontracting, and if you'll have another person supervising the job. It's also a good idea to discuss, up-front, your expected method of payment. If you end up submitting a bid and getting the job, a good contract and a solid understanding between you and the owner are key to a successful outcome for you both.

The Senior Client

Communication with older adults can be a little more challenging, partly because you need to define their specific needs (based on their individual level of independence or mobility), and also because adult children may be involved in the decision-making process. Design for seniors includes consideration of current and future living arrangements, style preferences, and the changes they may need in the years ahead if they plan to stay in their current home.

During Construction

When the project gets underway, the homeowner has a whole new set of stresses—disruption of their daily routine, lack of privacy, and being without parts of their house that they normally use every day. They may also have to OK additional expenses for unexpected work, or quickly make new product or design decisions if a planned item becomes unavailable or if existing conditions require another approach. Sometimes neighbors add to homeowners' stress by complaining about debris, trucks blocking their driveways, and dumpsters and stockpiled materials.

All of this will take place while your customers are attending to work, school, family, and the other demands of their daily lives. If you can make the project as painless as possible, and maybe even a pleasant experience, the job will go better for you, and you'll have the bonus of excellent references and referrals.

Some of the ways you can provide excellent customer service during construction:

- Prepare the owner with plenty of advance warning of upcoming tasks and disruptions. Be specific about when different types and phases of work will take place, who will be doing it, and what it will entail.

- Let your client know when major material deliveries, large trucks, and dumpsters will be arriving, so they can be prepared and let neighbors know what to expect.

- Remind the owner in advance of progress payments.

- Introduce household members to each of your crew members at the start of the job so they won't be surprised to find total strangers in the house.

- Address customer questions and concerns as soon as possible. Make sure your explanations are clearly understood so there won't be any surprises after work is in place.

- Immediately notify the owner of any unforeseen conditions and clarify extra costs. Then get their signature on change orders before you do the work.

- Maintain an orderly jobsite. At the end of each day, be sure it's swept up, and remove or at least unplug power tools, making sure they're out of the reach of children. Don't leave exposed nails or other materials that could cause injury.

- Make sure your employees honor any special requests the homeowner might make, such as not smoking or playing loud music in the house.

- Don't ask the homeowner to sign for your material deliveries. Only you are qualified to know if the order is correct.

Final Completion

In the last phase, homeowners will want to make sure that everything is complete as planned before they make their final payment. This phase will go a lot better for you and your customer if you've been communicating well throughout the project instead of waiting until the end to clear things up. If the homeowner made his/her expectations clear at the start, change orders were kept to a minimum, and the job stayed on schedule, the project should have a very good chance of a smooth wrap-up.

Before the project finish date, you'll want to go over all of the project's change orders, billings, and payments and prepare the final payment invoice. You'll also be inspecting the job to see what tasks still have to be completed before the final walk-through with the owner. When all the punch list items have been taken care of, you can review the final payment invoice with the owner and answer any last questions.

At the end of the project, as you receive your final payment, you'll be providing the owner with:

- Product information (including specific maintenance and care requirements) and warranties on cabinets, fixtures, appliances, and materials.

- Extra paint, tiles, and other materials for use in future repairs.

- Additional maintenance guidelines on other elements of the project (to help prevent call-backs for preventable damage).*

This is also a good time to take photos of the finished project for future presentations to potential customers. Don't forget to leave the owner with a few of your company business cards or brochures to pass along to friends or neighbors. A bouquet of flowers is also a nice gesture to help celebrate their new space.

See the National Association of Home Builders (NAHB) in the "Resources" section at the back of this book. NAHB publishes brochures that can be given to homeowners on how to care for their new space.

Remodeling Older Homes

There's no question that old houses, especially antique ones, have their own special character. You get the sense that any work you do should meet with the approval of the craftsmen who originally built them. A kitchen or bath renovation should introduce modern conveniences in a way that maintains the integrity of the architecture. You and the homeowner will need to decide how "pure" you want to be in terms of the design and the materials.

Some things to keep in mind when planning work on older homes:

- **"True" dimensional lumber.** This means that a 2 × 4 is actually 2" × 4", unlike today's 1-1/2" × 3-1/2" boards. This difference is consistent for all framing lumber. In old houses, the boards used for both rough and finish carpentry may be a full 1" thick, compared to today's 3/4" thick stock.

  If you're pursuing an exact restoration, you'll need to find a mill that produces the exact dimensional lumber you need. If exact reproduction isn't important, you'll have to use shims to build up narrower new members to match what's already in place. Where new members (both cosmetic and structural) will be exposed, true dimensional lumber will need to be used, and can be costly.

- **"Balloon-framing."** Vertical structural members (posts and studs) are continuous pieces from sill to roof plate. The intermediate floor joists are supported by ledger boards spiked to the studs. Temporary bracing and floor support may be needed when working on interior and exterior balloon-framed walls. Adding new wiring and utilities may be easier in a balloon-framed wall since the studs run uninterrupted from sill to roof plate, with the exception of fire stops.

- **Higher ceilings that require longer lengths of lumber for wall framing.** If the walls are over 8', you may need to allow for more waste when pricing wall finish materials. Load-bearing partition walls will require more re-framing material.

  In some cases, the original builder (or, later, a remodeler) may have placed additional blocking or bracing within the wall structure. This may obstruct the placement of new pipes or wiring, which could lead to additional demolition and re-framing.

- **Unique sizes and shapes of doors and windows.** Replacement may involve the services of a custom millwork company. Re-working old doors and sashes can be time-consuming. There may also be a long lead time for ordering custom units.

The different dimensions of framing members may result in varying wall thicknesses. Window and door frames may require extension jambs, adding to the cost and time of construction. Door and window frames that are part of the structural components may require special care during removal.

- **Built-in cabinets and shelves that may be tricky to remove.** This can involve a lot of patching and matching of finishes. Lath and plaster is generally thicker than drywall used today. To get a perfect finish, you may have to reconstruct and finish an entire wall.

- **Unique moldings** that may have to be custom-milled. When removing existing moldings and trim, determine the nailing pattern and fastening method that was used originally. Try to save as much material as possible. Even small pieces may come in handy for patching and replacing sections of trim, siding, moldings, or other details.

When you're trying to match existing materials, remove all layers of paint to establish true dimensions. Matching new trim to the old can also be difficult when the detail is hidden under many coats of paint. Hand-planed moldings, and those of the same shape but different size, may be costly to reproduce, but many stock moldings can be used in combination to produce a detail very similar to the original.

- **Unusual cornices and overhangs.** If you have to dismantle them, do so carefully to understand how they were put together, and to make patterns from the original pieces. Document the lengths of overhangs and flashing details so you can reproduce the look. Taking things apart carefully also lets you fabricate parts and do some of the assembly on the ground, rather than on a scaffold.

- **Period building components,** light fixtures, bath and kitchen fixtures, cabinetry, and hardware. Many companies specialize in reproducing these items in versions that will satisfy current building codes.

- **Structural/engineering concerns.** A professional engineer may need to be consulted on any structural issues, fireplace and chimney rebuilding, or complex electrical or plumbing problems.

- **Abatement of hazardous materials.** If your project will involve removal of hazardous items, such as asbestos pipe covering, a licensed specialist may be required.

The "Green Building" Trend

Green building is a major movement in both new home construction and remodeling. Builders, architects, and material suppliers are responding to consumers' growing interest in healthier, more comfortable houses with lower energy and water bills—not to mention building practices that support a healthy environment. New standards, such as LEED™ (Leadership in Energy and Environmental Design), ENERGY STAR® (for appliances and electronics), Greenspec® (for building materials and products), and the Forest Stewardship Council (lumber), have made it easier to identify and specify environmentally friendly building products.

Some green building features, such as integrated solar collection systems, super-efficient heating and air conditioning systems, and re-circulating hot water piping, are usually easier to build in as part of a new house. Many others, however, such as low-flow faucets and shower heads, thermal windows, fluorescent light fixtures, or whole-house fans, can easily be incorporated as part of another remodeling project.

Green Materials

Green building materials are those that:

- Are healthy for people. They don't produce indoor air quality problems in the home from harmful fumes or fibers, and they don't harm the workers who manufacture them.

- Are healthy for home use and the natural environment. They're better for people with chemical sensitivities. They don't degrade the environment or deplete scarce resources. They don't generate hazardous by-products or waste.

- Help minimize use of energy or water.

- Require little energy to manufacture.

- Are durable, reusable, recyclable, and/or biodegradable.

- Can be obtained locally to reduce fuel use for long-distance transportation.

What to Look For

Following are some examples of green building materials, products, and design approaches that your clients might want to consider incorporating in their remodeling projects. Some of these items are easier to find than others, but manufacturers are constantly expanding their offerings of environmentally friendly products. In some cases, green products may be a little more expensive initially, but the savings in energy or water use can pay back the investment very quickly.

- Appliances: Look for ENERGY STAR®-rated models.

- Brick and stone available locally.

- Cabinetry made with formaldehyde-free glues.

- Carpet and padding made of natural or recycled materials.

- Products for suspended ceilings: acoustic panels that are toxin-free, made of recycled materials.

- "Daylighting": placing windows to maximize natural light and views of the outdoors—to reduce eye strain and stress. Daylighting also means designing to diffuse or direct the light for best effect, and to avoid glare.

- Engineered wood products, made with smaller and faster-growing tree species. Products include finger-jointed lumber, glu-lam beams (which offer the advantage of extra strength over a long span), and pre-fabricated wood trusses and joists.

- Fireplaces: Consider radiant wood-burning stoves that burn cleaner and more efficiently.

- Flooring made of natural materials, such as bamboo, linoleum, and ceramic tile (made from recycled glass), cork, recycled rubber, or recycled or wool carpeting. (See also "Wood Flooring" below.)

- Floor finishes: water-based urethanes.

- Furniture and furnishings: Features to look for include ergonomic design, nontoxic materials, and sustainably harvested or recycled wood.

- High-efficiency heating, ventilating, cooling, and hot water systems. ENERGY STAR® ventilation/thermostats.

- Insulation with no, or low levels of irritants and pollutants. Cellulose and the new formaldehyde-free fiberglass products are reasonable choices. Purely natural materials include Perlite and cotton.

- Lighting: quality light fixtures and bulbs that minimize headaches and eye strain. Fluorescent fixtures and bulbs (including screw-in compact fluorescent bulbs) that maximize energy savings and last much longer. ENERGY STAR®-rated lighting.

- Paints: low- or no-VOC (volatile organic compounds) paints to minimize unhealthy air quality.

- Plumbing fixtures and faucets: low-flow models, re-circulating systems, and faucet aerators that use less water and/or energy.
- Recycling centers: storage (in a kitchen, pantry, mudroom, garage, or shed), to contain recyclables between pickups or drop-offs.
- Roofing: light-colored to reflect heat, insulated.
- Shingles: wood, plaster, and fiber cement.

- Thermal windows and doors: with the correct solar heat gain, heat loss, and visual transmittance values—both for your climate and for the orientation of the room to the sun.
- Water filtering systems: to improve the quality of your drinking water.
- Wood flooring that is recycled from old buildings, or new-growth (or new "certified") wood (www.certifiedwood.org).
- Wood sheathing made from recycled wood fibers.

You can also market your company's ability to recycle as much as possible of the waste if a project involves demolition. For example, old cabinets, windows, doors, or other items may be of interest to a salvage yard or community building recycling center.

For more information on green building, visit the following Web sites:

LEED™: www.usgbc.org

ENERGY STAR®: www.energystar.gov

Greenspec®: www.buildinggreen.com

Forest Stewardship Council: www.fscus.org

A Few Thoughts on Marketing

Marketing and sales follow a cycle—one phase leads to another. As a starting point, marketing (advertising, referrals) can be used to generate leads for new customers. Once you make contact with potential customers, you qualify them and possibly end up bidding a job for them. This may lead to signing a contract and getting the work. Next comes customer service. Exceptional service creates happy customers who come back with more projects and recommend the company to others, and the cycle starts again. Referrals are the lifeblood of any remodeling business.

Today the construction business is more competitive than ever. Not only are there more remodeling contractors, but they offer tremendous expertise and a variety of specialties. As the level of competition increases, so do the number of choices—and confusion—for homeowners. Without precise and defined differences, it can be difficult for customers to choose between one company and another.

Some of the main factors to think about in marketing are target markets, branding, co-branding, advertising, public relations, and customer service.

Target Markets

Successful remodeling companies focus their energies on the types of projects that are most profitable for their particular company. Some considerations are the size and type of project, geographic location, the type of customer, and the type of service you offer.

Branding

This is a consistent way of communicating who you are and what your values are to your customers—in all the ways you communicate—in any type of advertising and customer service. Branding can include a logo, slogan, or consistent image that you use in brochures, on your truck, on your company Web site, in a newsletter to customers, or on your invoices and contracts.

Branding can also mean communicating those same values in face-to-face meetings with customers and good customer service during the project. Developing your company "brand" is a way to tell customers what to expect from you and your company.

Your brand is not something contrived or candy-coated. It must reflect your true values. You want customers to think of quality, dependability, reliability, and trust when they think of you and your company. When customers are ready to begin a project, their decisions will be based on their perception of a company's value, which is defined as a combination of price and quality. Customers will trust you and your company when they feel a connection between their value systems and yours.

Co-Branding

This type of marketing involves linking your company's brand to another well-known brand, such as a product manufacturer. Industry leaders such as James Hardie, Kraftmaid, Kohler®, and Dupont Corian®, among others, offer excellent co-branding opportunities for remodelers. In co-branding programs, a manufacturer may help a builder who specifies its products with co-op advertising support, consumer-oriented brochures, design packages, and/or training.

Advertising

Contractors advertise in a number of ways, from signage on their trucks and project sites, to newspapers, the Yellow Pages, and on the Internet. These can all be important vehicles for placing your company in front of potential customers.

Your Web Site: An Important Advertising Tool

Drive around town and notice construction company trucks and signs. You'll probably see Web site addresses advertised as often as phone numbers. Web sites are one of the best forms of advertising because they allow you to explain your company's services and show photos of your most impressive projects. You can also display comments from satisfied customers, and other information on your company—its personnel, awards, community involvement, and achievements. Web sites also allow you to advertise your membership in professional associations, and give customers an easy way to contact you. You can update any of this information at any time.

Many builders set up their own Web sites. Others hire Web site designers to create and maintain their sites. Local chapters of professional associations, like the National Association of Home Builders, provide courses on Web site development for contractors. Community colleges and other adult education programs offer more general courses on Web site development. There are also many books available on Web site design.

The most successful sites give value to customers. For example, you can help them explore design options by providing links to product manufacturer Web sites. You can also post helpful information, such as guidelines from the National Kitchen and Bath Association on selecting bath fixtures, or maintenance how-to's for different materials.

Here are some tips for user-friendly Web sites:

- Avoid lengthy descriptions. Use brief, to-the-point statements.

- Stay away from large images that take too long to download.

- Keep the layout simple enough so users don't have to scroll to get to the information.

- Update the content regularly to keep it fresh and show your latest, best work.

Don't forget to publicize your Web site wherever you can—on your truck, on signs at your projects, and in brochures and advertisements.

Public Relations

This aspect of marketing involves making the public aware of your company—in the most favorable light possible. Good public relations can be one-on-one with your customers, in the form of quick responses to their questions and concerns, consideration of their comfort and privacy during construction, or a gift of flowers to celebrate completion of their new kitchen.

Public relations can also be more public... as in sponsoring community charities, taking a leading role in professional associations, and other efforts that generate "good press." Your reputation can make or break your success, so a positive image—based on solid work and community involvement—is crucial.

Customer Service

This is one of the most important aspects of your sales and marketing plan. Remodeling companies depend heavily on referrals from current and past customers. How these customers are treated, as well as how satisfied they are with the services provided to them, directly affects the flow and quality of referrals. No remodeling company can afford to buy each and every new customer through paid advertising.

Effective marketing can provide multiple benefits and rewards to a remodeler—from a better company image to access to more potential customers. The primary benefit of effective marketing is to increase both the quantity and quality of prospective clients, thereby boosting your business.

This segment is excerpted with permission from the National Association of Home Builders' (NAHB) University of Housing Sales and Marketing for Remodelers course. NAHB's Remodelors™ Council, representing 14,000 remodeling industry members, provides information, education, and designation programs to improve the business and construction expertise of its members and to enhance the professional image of the industry. "Remodelor" is the trademarked identifier of NAHB members active in the remodeling industry. For membership information, visit www.nahb.org/remodelors or call 800-368-5242 ext. 8217.

Closing the Sale— Understanding Cost Versus Value

Earning the homeowner's confidence in your knowledge and ability not only helps you win jobs, but can also help you expand a minor project into a full-scale remodel. Understanding—and being able to explain—the value of various improvements is an essential part of your sales effort.

While most homeowners who want to remodel are driven by the desire for more or better space, they also want to know that they'll gain a good return on their investment by adding to their home's resale value. You can look at this in a couple of ways: how many dollars the improvement adds to the home's selling price, and whether it's likely to help attract buyers if and when they put the house on the market.

Another dollar value measure is how much money the improvement will save them over time—in the form of lower utility bills. Examples are replacing plumbing fixtures or appliances with more efficient models.

You can also remind the homeowner of the other factors that influence value, such as:

- Quality of workmanship and materials.
- Appropriateness of the improvement in terms of style and design. (They should think neutral if they're planning to sell fairly soon, and the improvement should always be in harmony with the rest of the house.)
- Condition of the house overall.
- Selling prices of surrounding homes.

Studies by realtors and other industry organizations show that kitchen and bath improvements have the best payback when homes are sold. If the room has worn surfaces or an outdated look, an upgrade will have even more impact on improving the home's value.

Features to Include for Added Value

In addition to keeping the new space in line with the home's character and style, it helps to aim for certain popular, long-term trends in renovations.

For kitchens, focus on functional items such as counter space, dual sinks, and cooktop stoves, along with cosmetic improvements such as stainless appliances, attractive countertops and backsplashes, and current light fixtures, including under-cabinet lighting. If the homeowner wants to add space, a pantry or eating area is valued. Kitchens and family rooms should maximize natural light.

Current bath trends also include lots of natural light; neutral, clean colors and materials; and visual expansion of space. Ceramic tile floors and partial walls continue to be sought after, along with attractive fixtures and faucets, and lighting.

See the introductions to the "Kitchens" and "Baths" project estimate sections for design tips and guidelines.

Part Two

Kitchens

Kitchen Remodeling

This section of the book is made up of estimates for sample kitchen projects. Each project estimate comes with:

- A materials list with unit and total costs*
- Typical labor-hours (contractor and subcontractors) for the tasks involved
- Total cost, including overhead and profit*
- Some things to consider if you're planning a similar job
- Floor plans showing the layout of the model project that was estimated
- And, for most whole-room renovations, a blank Project Worksheet that you can use to list, count, and price the items needed for your particular jobs

Use the "Location Factors" at the back of the book to easily adjust costs to your specific location.

Refer to these estimates for quick, rough prices for preliminary discussions with a homeowner. Or, use them as a "sanity check" to make sure your detailed estimates are "in the ballpark" and have accounted for all the major items and tasks.

Following is a quick review of kitchen components with some tips on materials and installation. Much of this information is based on National Kitchen & Bath Association (NKBA) recommendations.

Cabinets

Usually the most expensive item in a kitchen remodel. Customers who aren't working with designers may need your guidance in selecting cabinets within their budget. Collect manufacturer catalogs and prices so you're up-to-date on what's available.

Stock, Semi-Custom, or Custom

Stock cabinets are either immediately available or can usually be ordered for delivery within a few weeks. Quality ranges widely, so check their features and workmanship.

Semi-custom cabinets, in stock sizes, let the customer choose different door and drawer styles and finishes. They usually take about eight weeks for delivery.

Custom cabinets' biggest issues are price and long lead times. Work with your customer on timely selection, then stay in close touch with the supplier once the cabinets are ordered to make sure *all* of the cabinets, *as specified*, will be delivered on time to avoid a major glitch in the overall project schedule.

Framed Versus Frameless

With framed cabinets, the frame shows around the doors. Frameless cabinet doors cover the frames for a sleeker look. Framed cabinet construction provides more stability than frameless units. However, the resulting smaller openings affect the size of drawers and roll-out shelves.

Frameless cabinets form a box, don't require a front frame for stability or squareness, and have larger door and drawer openings. The drawbacks are the need for careful planning (and sometimes the use of fillers) to make sure you have proper door clearances.

Types of Cabinets, Accessories, & Hardware

When you order cabinets and/or draw up a plan, you'll be defining the type of unit and showing its location and special features. Cabinet types include base, wall, corner, peninsula corner, appliance garages, microwave cabinets, and pantry cabinets. Accessories include drawers (with cutlery/silverware trays, bread boxes, and spice racks); pull-out shelves, cutting boards, towel racks, and bins (wastebasket, recycling, vegetable, etc.); lazy susans; tilt-out trays (at sink front); plate and wine racks; special shelving (open and on inside face of cabinet doors); glass doors; extended stiles (to fill in extra space between wall and cabinet); moldings; and matching panels for appliances.

A standard quality of hardware generally comes with stock cabinets. If the homeowner does not like the choices, some vendors will deduct the cost, allowing the owner to purchase hardware elsewhere. If they choose metal (especially brass) pulls and knobs, but from different manufacturers, compare the two to be sure they are the same color and finish.

Cabinet Materials
Steel

There are two categories: economy models painted various colors, and high-end stainless steel units often selected for high-tech kitchens. Economy models may not be the best choice for the homeowner who wants to increase the home's resale value, and they are susceptible to rust.

Laminate on Particleboard

Common in economy to moderate kitchen remodels. "Low-pressure" laminates ("melamine") are cheaper, but more susceptible to impact damage. "High-pressure" laminates are as durable as laminate countertops, but more expensive. Vinyl and foil films are less durable. Good warranties are important in case of de-lamination or other wear issues. Often available, in limited selections, from discount outlets.

Hardwood

Usually oak, cherry, or maple, these cabinets are popular for their quality, appearance, ease of maintenance, and durability. Moderate to high price, but considered a good investment in the home's resale value.

Hardboard

Also known as Hard Density Fiberboard (HDF) or "Masonite," these cabinets are durable and easy to maintain. Moderate cost and return on investment.

Installation Tips

Clearances

- If you're installing cabinets that will go up to the ceiling, make sure that fully open doors will clear any ceiling lights (with the bulbs in place). If you can allow an inch or more between the ceiling and the top of the cabinet, this will help with clearances, and you can cover the gap with crown molding.
- Any cabinets that will sit directly on the counter (such as the upper part of a china cabinet-type unit) should have a 3/4" to 1-1/2" buffer piece in between to prevent the cabinet doors from resting directly on the counter.

- For drawers that are adjacent to a door or window, use a filler piece to maintain enough clearance between the open drawer and the casing.
- Allow space for cabinet doors to open completely if you have pull-out shelves or bins.

Moldings

Use batten molding to hide joints between cabinets, outside corner molding to cover the joint where two cabinets meet at right angles, and scribe molding at an uneven ceiling.

Re-Facing Cabinets

This can be a good strategy for homeowners whose budget can't accommodate new cabinets. While it's possible to purchase re-facing materials at some home centers, this job may be better subcontracted to a specialist. If you don't specialize in this work, making old cabinets "like-new" can be difficult and more time-consuming than it might seem, and there's a risk of call-backs as they continue to wear.

Countertops

Precise measuring is key to on-budget, on-schedule countertop installations. Also, be sure to clarify the backsplash height and material in advance. Special backsplash materials like glass tiles and stamped stainless steel may take time for the homeowner to select, and to special order.

Materials

Laminate

Inexpensive, durable, and with a huge range of pattern and color options (including faux stone types) and wood and other edge treatments. Laminate is stain-resistant and waterproof, but can be damaged by a hot pot or scratched, and there's no effective way to repair it. It comes in widths from 18"-60". About $30 per LF, installed, without wood trim, but including backsplash. Wood edging can add roughly $10-$15 per LF of countertop.

Laminate is adhered to 3/4" plywood or particleboard, with a frame that keeps it rigid and attaches to the cabinets at the perimeter and at countertop seams.

Solid Surface (e.g., Dupont Corian® and Silestone®)

This material is durable and also heatproof and waterproof, with the advantages of integrated sinks and a variety of edge treatments. About $120 per LF installed.

Solid surface counters are typically installed by the fabricator. Any seams where pieces are joined should be nearly invisible. Overhangs of 1/2" material should not be more than 6" without support, 12" for 3/4" material. It's generally recommended that solid surface counters "float" on the substrate material, with a perimeter frame and an 18" OC web support system. Allow a clearance of 1/8" minimum from the wall for expansion of the material when heated. Biscuit splines (usually three per joint) are often used to ensure proper alignment of joined sections. One is in the middle of the joint, and each of the others is about 3" from the outside edge.

Granite & Other Stone

Stone counters are popular despite their expense for the high-end look and as an investment in a home's resale value. In addition to granite, there are limestone, soapstone, slate, travertine, engineered quartz, and concrete, among others.

Most are durable, waterproof, and heatproof, but can chip. Be sure the surface is sealed (unless it's engineered stone) to prevent staining, and, as with all materials, provide the homeowner with maintenance instructions. About $150 per LF, installed.

Since granite countertops are prefabricated by the vendor and cannot be adjusted on-site, accurate measurements are crucial. Typical thicknesses are 3/4" and 1-1/4". The latter is recommended since, at relatively modest extra cost, its strength can support up to a 12" overhang, and it's more resistant to breakage when transported and installed. Make sure the frame system will support the weight.

Granite is usually available in slabs up to 4.6' x 9'. If two pieces will be joined, they should be matched for color and consistency in the grain pattern. Seams should be in the least noticeable locations like where cut-outs are made, but not around the sink (to prevent moisture penetration).

Ceramic Tile

Glazed tile is very durable—heatproof and waterproof, and resistant to scratches and stains. The grout can stain though, especially if it's a light color. Re-grouting may be necessary at some point in the future, depending on how much wear the counter gets. About $45 per LF for mid-priced tile, installed.

Be sure to select the right type of tile for the installation, e.g., decorative with painted or relief patterns for the backsplash (where detail won't wear), and make sure edge and trim pieces are available for the countertop.

Tile is set on a deck using mastic, mud, or thin set. The decking lumber should be on-site at least a few days in advance so it can acclimate to the humidity in the space. If you're planning an overhang, make sure there's a rigid base for the tile to avoid cracking.

Stainless Steel

This material is waterproof, heatproof, can be cleaned to a shine, and will not corrode. The downsides are the high price and susceptibility to scratching.

Wood

Often used on an island, wood is durable with proper care, but usually requires annual re-sealing. About $75 per LF. The type of finish will depend on the homeowner's planned use for the surface. Also, if you need to cut and fit the piece on-site, plan to use unfinished wood for a better installation.

When choosing a finish, make sure that the product is nontoxic and approved for contact with food. Some brands of polyurethane meet this criteria. Check the manufacturer's label or consult your paint supplier. Another option is to use mineral oil, tung oil, or another natural oil that is safe for food contact. The homeowner will need to reapply these oils at regular intervals, depending on how often the counter is used and cleaned.

Wood countertops are warm, durable, and easy to refinish, but can stain or burn easily and are susceptible to water damage if the homeowner is not careful.

Countertop Design Guidelines:

- At least 36" of continuous countertop for each work area, and at least one work area next to the sink.

- At least 9" of countertop on one side of the cooktop, with 15" minimum counter on the other side.

- At least 15" of counter space next to or across from (no more than 48" away) the refrigerator.

- Use corbel brackets to support counter extensions on base cabinets. If the overhang is greater than 12", a support bracket is recommended at 36" intervals. (Consult the manufacturer or fabricator for required support for solid surface, granite, and other stone countertop overhangs.)

Flooring

Vinyl

Economical, but customers should choose the best grade their budget allows, due to the high traffic on kitchen floors. If they select a wood or stone pattern, it should have as little repeat as possible. About $5.50 per SF for sheet vinyl, $3.50 per SF for vinyl tiles.

Linoleum

Popular once again because it's made from natural or "green" materials, linoleum should also be chosen in a quality grade with a good warranty.

Ceramic, Quarry, or Stone Tile

Some of the options include a slip-resistant finish, and glazed versus unglazed tile. (Glazed is less porous and more stain-resistant.) Darker grout makes it easier to maintain. Stone tile needs to be sealed to prevent stains.

You'll need an adequate sub floor to support the weight of stone or ceramic tiles. About $8 per SF for quarry or ceramic tile.

Wood

Wood flooring is typically coated with polyurethane for moisture protection. Make sure the customer is aware of the qualities of different wood species, and the maintenance requirements and wear issues before they select their flooring. About $9 per SF for oak strip flooring. *(See the New Flooring & Wall/Ceiling Finishes project for more on types of flooring.)*

"Floating" Laminate Floors

Laminate flooring resembles wood and offers durability in a kitchen or bath. Warranties vary based on the construction of the material. Laminate flooring can often be installed over existing floors. About $6 per SF.

Appliances

Make sure you're clear on the exact models and dimensions of all appliances, and allow adequate clearance for them between cabinets and walls.

See the Baths section for guidance on sinks, as well as more on countertops and flooring.

Cabinet Re-Facing

Replace cabinet doors and drawer fronts. Apply matching face veneer and new hardware.

This project estimate is for re-facing existing kitchen cabinet bodies with a layer of wood veneer and then adding new cabinet doors, drawer fronts, hinges, and pulls or knobs. While this work is often subcontracted out to services that specialize in it, the parts are available (in limited styles) at many home centers.

If the existing cabinets are unusual sizes or configurations, custom doors and drawer fronts can be made by a millwork shop, at a higher cost. Custom millwork also offers the homeowner

options such as adding a specific type of crown molding, or improving drawer configurations (for example, replacing two narrow drawers with one larger one).

If the kitchen has available space, the homeowner might also want to consider adding cabinets—either identical to or coordinating with the re-faced cabinets. Another option is adding interior cabinet upgrades, such as sliding shelves and bins.

This model project estimate covers 25 LF of base cabinets and 20 LF of upper cabinets, and is based on

hardwood cabinet doors and drawer fronts and hardwood veneer plywood materials. Stained or painted wood doors (with wood veneer covering for cabinet bodies) might also be used, generally at a higher cost.

Homeowners with a limited budget might prefer to save money by having the existing cabinets painted, and the hardware upgraded. See the "Alternates" box for a cost estimate for this more modest "facelift" for the same size kitchen. (The painting estimate is for the exterior of the cabinets only.)

Project Estimate

Description	Quantity		Labor		Cost per Unit		Total Cost		
	Quantity	Unit	Labor Hrs Per Unit	Labor Hrs Total	Material Per Unit	Installation Per Unit	Material Total	Installation Total	Total
Self-Performed									
Remove cabinet doors and drawer fronts	24	Ea.	0.12	2.88		3.57		86	86
Hardwood raised panel base cabinet doors	10	Ea.	0.55	5.50	45	22.50	450	225	675
Hardwood raised panel wall cabinet doors	14	Ea.	0.57	7.98	49.50	23.50	693	329	1,022
Hardwood base cabinet drawer fronts	10	Ea.	0.57	5.70	33.50	23.50	335	235	570
Hardwood plywood end panels	32	S.F.	0.04	1.28	3.19	1.63	102	52	154
Face frame veneer strips	32	S.F.	0.04	1.28	3.19	1.63	102	52	154
Cabinet drawer pulls	10	Ea.	0.05	0.50	4.17	2.04	42	20	62
Cabinet door pulls	24	Ea.	0.08	1.92	5.55	3.42	133	82	215
Cabinet door hinges	24	Pr.	0.12	2.88	8.40	4.79	202	115	317
Subtotals							2,059	1,196	3,255
General Requirements (Site Overhead)						12%	247	144	391
Subtotals							2,306	1,340	3,646
Overhead and Profit						10%	231	134	365
Subtotals							2,537	1,474	4,011

Grand Total $4,011

Alternates

	Unit	Total Cost
Painting facelift		
Paint cabinets	S.F.	$1
New door pulls	Ea.	$6
New drawer pulls	Ea.	$6
New hinges	Pr.	$13

Cabinet Door Styles

Raised
"Cathedral" Panel

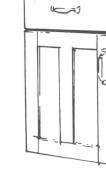

Double
Recessed Panel

Recessed Panel

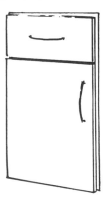

Flat or "Slab"

Sink & Countertop Facelift

> *Remove old countertop and sink. Install solid surface counter with integrated sink and faucet.*

If the existing cabinets are in good shape, and the homeowner is happy with the layout, this project is a fairly economical way to upgrade and update the kitchen. New countertops can also be designed with a slightly different edge or overhang to improve the look and function of an island, or the room's traffic flow. A sink older than ten years may well be worn or lack convenience features.

Measuring for countertops is a crucial operation. Even a minor mistake can be costly and schedule-busting if a whole unit has to be scrapped.

Solid surface countertops with integrated sinks, like the one estimated for this project, simplify the decision-making and are easy to maintain. Many contractors fabricate their own laminate countertops.

Drop-in sink choices include stainless, cast iron, enameled steel, stone, and porcelain. Avoid light-gauge stainless, which can bend if connected to a garbage disposal. Make sure the homeowner is educated on all the pros and cons (maintenance, durability, costs) of the sink and faucet materials and models they're considering. Be sure to clarify in advance any extras, such as soap dispensers, sprayers, instant hot water dispensers, and water filtration systems.

As long as the new sink will go in the same location as the old one, the plumbing should be straightforward—provided there are working shut-off valves. Care is needed in removing the old sink to avoid breaking or crimping water supply piping. If an older home

has galvanized pipe for the existing drain, it should be replaced with plastic piping to avoid future problems with rust and grease buildup.

This project estimate covers the costs to remove an old sink and countertop and install a new solid surface counter with an integral sink. See the "Alternates" box for costs to add a garbage disposal and for different kinds of sinks (cast iron, medium-gauge stainless, or porcelain) and faucets. Costs are also given for different countertop materials (laminate, granite, marble, and stainless steel), and for backsplash options (laminate, tile, and stainless steel).

Project Estimate

Description	Quantity		Labor		Cost per Unit		Total Cost		
	Quantity	Unit	Labor Hrs Per Unit	Labor Hrs Total	Material Per Unit	Installation Per Unit	Material Total	Installation Total	Total
Self-Performed									
Remove existing countertop	13	L.F.	0.08	1.04		2.36		31	31
Solid surface kitchen counter	13	L.F.	0.80	10.40	65	32.50	845	423	1,268
Solid surface kitchen sink	1	Ea.	4	4	440	163	440	163	603
Remove debris	1	C.Y.	0.67	0.67		19.65		20	20
Subcontract									
Remove existing sink	1	Ea.	1.14	1.14		50.50		51	51
Kitchen sink rough-in	1	Ea.	7.48	7.48	115	298	115	298	413
Install kitchen faucet	1	Ea.	0.80	0.80	56.50	35.50	57	36	93
Subtotals							1,457	1,022	2,479
General Requirements (Site Overhead)						12%	175	123	297
Subtotals							1,632	1,145	2,776
Overhead and Profit						10%	163	115	278
Subtotals							1,795	1,260	3,054

Grand Total $3,054

Alternates

	Unit	Total Cost
Countertop materials		
Plastic laminate	L.F.	$39
Marble	L.F.	$114
Maple butcher block	L.F.	$80
Granite	L.F.	$147
Ceramic tile	L.F.	$42
Stainless steel	S.F.	$146
Kitchen sinks		
Single bowl porcelain enamel on cast iron	Ea.	$340
Double bowl porcelain enamel on cast iron	Ea.	$450
Single bowl stainless steel	Ea.	$520
Double bowl stainless steel	Ea.	$810
Single bowl enameled steel	Ea.	$235
Double bowl enameled steel	Ea.	$294
Accessories		
Garbage disposal	Ea.	$205
Single control lever handle faucet, with pull-out spray, white	Ea.	$238
Single control lever handle faucet, with pull-out spray, polished chrome	Ea.	$219
Single control lever handle faucet, with pull-out spray, polished brass	Ea.	$256
Backsplash options		
Plastic laminate	S.F.	$6
Ceramic tile	S.F.	$8
Stainless steel	S.F.	$7

New Flooring & Wall/Ceiling Finishes

Tear out old resilient flooring and replace with hardwood. Paint walls and ceiling.

A new hardwood floor, wall, and ceiling finishes are exciting and relatively painless projects for homeowners, since these improvements have a major impact on a kitchen's appearance, but don't take the space out of service for very long. Important considerations for estimating and scheduling this work include educating the homeowner on the various flooring material options, allowing ample lead time for special order materials, and evaluating the old flooring for potential complications in its removal.

If the old flooring is thin, such as sheet vinyl, and the new hardwood planks will be installed on top of the existing (or same thickness) underlayment, thresholds will be required to transition to the new height wherever the kitchen meets adjoining spaces.

Be sure to caution homeowners about ventilation requirements and drying times—and the need to vacate the premises altogether following application of volatile stains, varnishes, or polyurethanes. Also, be sure to give homeowners detailed instructions and warranty requirements from the manufacturer or distributor for properly maintaining their new flooring once it's installed.

This project estimate includes removal of the old sheet vinyl flooring and underlayment in a 9' 6" × 10' 6" room, preparation of walls and ceiling for painting, and installation of new underlayment, followed by hardwood strip flooring—including sanding and finishing.

The "Alternates" box provides costs per square foot for some other popular flooring options including "floating" laminate (e.g., Pergo®), sheet vinyl, linoleum (getting popular again because of its natural ingredients), and 12" × 12" ceramic and limestone tiles.

Project Estimate

Description	Quantity	Unit	Labor Hrs Per Unit	Labor Hrs Total	Material Per Unit	Installation Per Unit	Material Total	Installation Total	Total
Self-Performed									
Remove sheet vinyl flooring	1	Job	2	2		59		59	59
Remove flooring underlayment	1	Job	2	2		59		59	59
Prep gypsum wallboard surfaces for painting	320	S.F.				0.09		29	29
Remove demolished materials	1	C.Y.	0.97	0.97		28.50		29	29
Hardwood strip flooring	85	S.F.	0.05	4.25	3.30	1.92	281	163	444
Sand and finish flooring	85	S.F.	0.03	2.55	0.76	0.80	65	68	133
Prime and paint gypsum wallboard, 2 coats	320	S.F.	0.01	3.20	0.16	0.44	51	141	192
Subtotals							397	548	945
General Requirements (Site Overhead)						12%	48	66	113
Subtotals							445	614	1,058
Overhead and Profit						10%	45	61	106
Subtotals							490	675	1,164

Grand Total $1,164

Alternates

Flooring	Unit	Total Cost
Floating laminate flooring	S.F.	$6
Sheet vinyl flooring	S.F.	$5
Linoleum flooring	S.F.	$6
12" x 12" ceramic tile flooring	S.F.	$6
Stone flooring	S.F.	$43

A quick review of wood flooring styles and types:

Strip—usually 2-1/4" wide, with tongue-and-groove and matching ends and edges.

Plank—different widths, may include wood or simulated wood plugs.

Parquet—squares of glued wood pieces in patterns.

Hardwoods—Oak, beech, birch, maple, heart pine, ash, Brazilian cherry (hardest and most dent-resistant), and pecan. Douglas fir is considered a hardwood, though it's softer than the others.

Soft woods—Pine, fir, and hemlock.

Lighting & Electrical Upgrade

Install new chandelier, recessed, pendant, and under-cabinet fixtures, and run wiring for speakers and computer.

Lighting should be considered in the early planning stages of a kitchen renovation. Specialty fixtures may have long lead times, so it's important to get homeowners started on decision-making well in advance. Creating a lighting plan—and a wiring plan for a desk computer and speakers—requires first establishing the layout of all of the kitchen's main components.

Good lighting is key to a kitchen's function and appearance, and is determined by a combination of natural window light and electrical *ambient* (or *general*), *task*, and *accent* lighting. Ambient lighting can come from a central ceiling fixture or a combination of a central fixture with recessed ceiling lights.

Task lighting focuses on work areas such as a baking counter, stove, sink, or island. Task light fixtures can be recessed down-lights, under-cabinet lights, or track or pendant lighting over the island.

Accent lights—usually recessed, wall-mounted, or track fixtures—can highlight a kitchen's special features, such as ornate moldings or artwork. Inside-cabinet lights can also be used as accents to spotlight a china collection behind glass doors.

This project estimate covers the installation of a new chandelier, two recessed light fixtures, and under-cabinet lighting, as well as two pendant light fixtures and an added GFI outlet. Also included are two light switches and a dimmer for the recessed lights.

The estimate also includes installation of speaker wiring and box covers, and computer coaxial cable, as well as cutting out and patching of gypsum wallboard and fishing wires as needed.

Project Estimate

Description	Quantity	Unit	Labor Hrs Per Unit	Labor Hrs Total	Material Per Unit	Installation Per Unit	Material Total	Installation Total	Total
Self-Performed									
Cut out gypsum wallboard for wire installation	10	Ea.	0.33	3.30		9.80		98	98
Patch gypsum wallboard	10	Ea.	0.73	7.30	0.07	29.50	1	295	296
Subcontract									
Fish wire to new lighting	4	Ea.	0.25	1	4.87	11.10	19	44	63
Fish wire to new GFI outlet	1	Ea.	0.25	0.25	4.87	11.10	5	11	16
Fish computer coaxial cable to new connection	1	Ea.	0.50	0.50	13.90	22	14	22	36
Fish speaker wire to new connection	1	Ea.	0.31	0.31	8.10	13.70	8	14	22
New chandelier	1	Ea.	1.33	1.33	330	59.50	330	60	390
Recessed lighting	2	Ea.	1	2	93.50	44.50	187	89	276
Under-cabinet lighting	5	Ea.	1.14	5.70	86.50	51	433	255	688
Pendant lighting fixtures	2	Ea.	0.40	0.80	129	17.80	258	36	294
Switches	2	Ea.	0.20	0.40	5.30	8.90	11	18	29
Dimmer switch	1	Ea.	0.50	0.50	11.90	22	12	22	34
Plastic junction boxes	14	Ea.	0.35	4.90	3.78	15.45	53	216	269
GFI receptacle	1	Ea.	0.30	0.30	32.50	13.15	33	13	46
Switch, cable, and speaker box covers	5	Ea.	0.10	0.50	0.34	4.45	2	22	24
Subtotals							1,366	1,215	2,581
General Requirements (Site Overhead)						12%	164	146	310
Subtotals							1,530	1,361	2,891
Overhead and Profit						10%	153	136	289
Subtotals							1,683	1,497	3,180

Grand Total   **$3,180**

Kitchen Wiring and Electrical

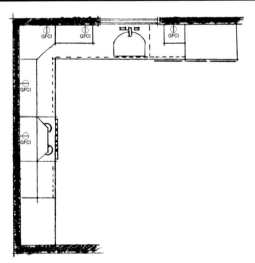

Code Requirement:
* GFCI (Ground-fault circuit-interrupter) protection is required on all receptacles servicing countertop surfaces within the kitchen. (IRC E 3802.6)

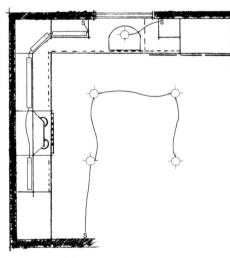

Recommended:
In addition to general lighting required by code, every work surface should be well illuminated by appropriate task lighting.

Code Requirement:
* At least one wall-switch controlled light must be provided. Switch must be placed at the entrance. (IRC E 3803.2)

Based on guidelines published by the National Kitchen & Bath Association

Basic Kitchen Island Unit

Install island cabinet and solid surface countertop.

Half of all new kitchens have island units, according to the National Kitchen & Bath Association (NKBA). An island can add valuable work and storage space, and improve the layout of the work triangle (sink/refrigerator/stove).

Many islands are 30"-36" deep, allowing for cabinets or drawers on both sides. Custom units can address unique space requirements, provided there is ample clearance for traffic flow and opening cabinet and appliance doors.

A current trend is to have one or two cabinet components with a different finish from the others, as accents. For example, you might have a stained wood island with a granite countertop that coordinates with painted wood wall cabinets with solid color laminate countertops.

This project estimate is for the installation of a 30" × 48" island, comprised of a stock base cabinet with two doors and two drawers. The island countertop is solid surface material.

The "Alternates" box includes costs for a granite countertop, the addition of electrical outlets, and a downdraft cooktop.

Project Estimate

Description	Quantity		Labor		Cost per Unit		Total Cost		
	Quantity	Unit	Labor Hrs Per Unit	Labor Hrs Total	Material Per Unit	Installation Per Unit	Material Total	Installation Total	Total
Self-Performed									
Base cabinet, 30" x 48", two doors, two drawers	2	Ea.	0.85	1.70	380	34.50	760	69	829
Solid surface material island top	8	L.F.	0.80	6.40	65	32.50	520	260	780
Subtotals							1,280	329	1,609
General Requirements (Site Overhead)						12%	154	39	193
Subtotals							1,434	368	1,802
Overhead and Profit						10%	143	37	180
Subtotals							1,577	405	1,982

Grand Total $1,982

Alternates

	Unit	Total Cost
Islands		
Granite countertop	L.F.	$147
Duplex electrical outlets	Ea.	$32
Downdraft cooktop with burners and grill/griddle	Ea.	$825
Electrical connection for above	Job	$89
Ductwork for above	L.F.	$5

Deluxe Kitchen Island Unit

Install island cabinet with solid surface countertop, integrated sink, and GFI outlets.

Most new and remodeled larger kitchens have island units. Even in smaller kitchen renovations, islands can often be fit in—either as a divider to the adjoining breakfast, family, or dining room, or in the center of the kitchen with some creative shaping and sizing to ensure good traffic flow.

The newest trends for island units, especially in higher-end kitchens, are furniture-quality wood cabinet bases with details such as turned posts and fluted columns, and decorative sinks in unusual shapes.

The estimate for this project includes installation of two 30" × 48" hardwood base cabinets with doors and drawers on one side. The island has a solid surface countertop with an integrated vegetable sink. Two GFI duplex outlets are also priced, allowing for up to 20' of wiring for each.

Since many homeowners want to tailor their kitchen island toward entertaining, we've included costs for an under-counter wine refrigerator, a bar sink, and an instant hot water dispenser in the "Alternates" box. Costs are also given for a decorative combination chandelier/pot rack, for granite and maple butcher block countertop options, and for a dishwasher, including rough-in and installation.

Project Estimate

Description	Quantity		Labor		Cost per Unit		Total Cost		
	Quantity	Unit	Labor Hrs Per Unit	Labor Hrs Total	Material Per Unit	Installation Per Unit	Material Total	Installation Total	Total
Self-Performed									
Base cabinet, 30" x 48", two doors, two drawers	2	Ea.	0.85	1.70	380	34.50	760	69	829
Solid surface island top	8	L.F.	0.80	6.40	65	32.50	520	260	780
Solid surface vegetable sink	1	Ea.	1.76	1.76	203	71.50	203	72	275
Subcontract									
Plumbing rough-in	1	Ea.	.48	.48	115	298	115	298	413
Vegetable sink faucet	1	Ea.	0.80	0.80	56.50	35.50	57	36	93
GFI duplex outlets	2	Ea.	0.65	1.30	38.50	29	77	58	135
Subtotals							1,732	793	2,525
General Requirements (Site Overhead)						12%	208	95	303
Subtotals							1,940	888	2,828
Overhead and Profit						10%	194	89	283
Subtotals							2,134	977	3,111

Grand Total $3,111

Alternates

Deluxe Islands	Unit	Total Cost
Wine refrigerator	Ea.	$1,050
Bar sink with faucet and fittings	Ea.	$167
Rough plumbing for above	Ea.	$415
Instant hot water dispenser	Ea.	$160
Decorative combination chandelier/pot rack	Ea.	$585
Rough electric for above	Job	$89
Granite countertop	L.F.	$147
Maple butcher block countertop	L.F.	$80
Dishwasher	Ea.	$820
Rough plumbing for above	Ea.	$375
Rough electric for above	Job	$89

Kitchen Eating Area

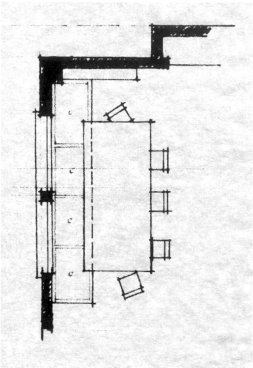

Frame, install, and trim new casement and half-round windows. Build and finish built-in bench.

This project provides a space-maximizing kitchen eating area, together with a new decorative casement with half-round window to brighten and customize the space. If the existing kitchen doesn't have room for the banquette seating estimated in this project, a bump-out might be a way to gain enough extra space.

The most common arrangement for informal eat-in kitchen areas is a free-standing table and chairs—often called the "breakfast nook." If there isn't enough space for a table, and an island with counter stools isn't an option, there may be room for a banquette or booth consisting of built-in benches and a built-in or free-standing table.

The term "booth" is often confused with "banquette," which is actually a built-in straight or L-shaped bench with a table and chairs on the other side. Banquettes are space-saving, but booths tend to be the most compact, as they fit tightly into corners. Benches can be plain wood or upholstered, or can even contain storage units.

If you are building a booth, the measurement allowances are usually 12" of vertical clearance between the tabletop and seat, and an 18" seat height. The front edges of the benches typically extend 3"–4" under the table. The benches should be the same length as the table.

In addition to building and painting the banquette bench, this project estimate covers the demolition for, and installation of, the new window. This includes patching the siding and installing the exterior and interior trim.

Project Estimate

Description	Quantity		Labor		Cost per Unit		Total Cost		
	Quantity	Unit	Labor Hrs Per Unit	Labor Hrs Total	Material Per Unit	Installation Per Unit	Material Total	Installation Total	Total
Self-Performed									
Exterior demolition	1	Job	2	2		81.50		82	82
Interior demolition	1	Job	2	2		81.50		82	82
Frame new window opening	60	L.F.	0.03	1.80	0.37	1.30	22	78	100
Window header	10	L.F.	0.05	0.50	1.76	2.17	18	22	40
4' x 3'-6" casement window	1	Ea.	0.94	0.94	500	38.50	500	39	539
Half-round window	1	Ea.	2.67	2.67	530	109	530	109	639
Patch siding	1	Job	2	2		81.50		82	82
Trim, interior casing, stock pine, 11/16" x 2-1/2"	33	L.F.	0.03	0.99	0.94	1.36	31	45	76
Putty and prime interior trim	33	L.F.	0.01	0.33	0.03	0.44	1	15	16
Paint interior trim, 2 coats	33	L.F.	0.01	0.33	0.03	0.44	1	15	16
Caulking	32	L.F.	0.03	0.96	0.17	1.33	5	43	48
Bench framing	80	L.F.	0.03	2.40	0.37	1.30	30	104	134
Bench top	20	S.F.	0.07	1.40	5.30	2.91	106	58	164
Bench top trim	14	L.F.			4.29		60		60
Bench base covering	30	S.F.	0.02	0.60	0.28	0.68	8	20	28
Bench & trim staining	52	S.F.	0.01	0.52	0.05	0.48	3	25	28
Bench & trim finishing	52	S.F.	0.03	1.56	0.19	1.04	10	54	64
Subtotals							1,325	873	2,198
General Requirements (Site Overhead)						12%	159	105	264
Subtotals							1,484	978	2,462
Overhead and Profit						10%	148	98	246
Subtotals							1,632	1,076	2,708

Grand Total   **$2,708**

Other Dining Options & Space Requirements

Free-Standing Table with Chairs:
- Allow about 12-15 SF and at least 21" of table space for each person who will be seated at the table. This is at least 48 SF for four people.

- Find out if the homeowner will be using table extensions when planning the space.

- Allow at least 32" from the table to the nearest wall if one or more chairs will be used on the wall side.

Counter with Stools
- Standard height is 36" with 24" stools. Bar height is 42" with 30" minimum stool height.

- Allow at least 21" of counter space per person, and 24" of knee space.

Lighting
Dining areas should have a warm, comfortable atmosphere with lower-level lighting, whereas homework or paperwork requires bright task lighting. Make sure the homeowner considers all uses of the area when selecting lighting for it. Dimmer switches will help address this issue.

"Bed & Breakfast" Gas Fireplace

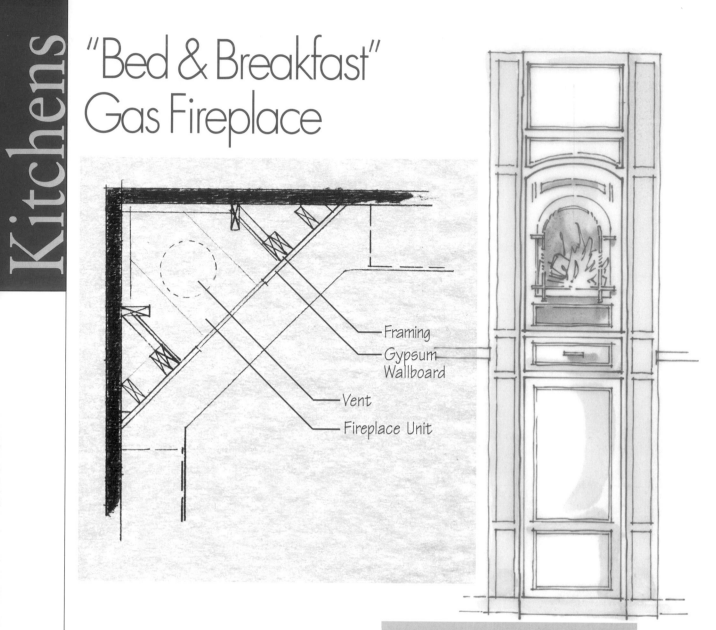

Framing
Gypsum Wallboard
Vent
Fireplace Unit

Frame, rough-in gas piping and electrical wiring, and install prefabricated fireplace and vents.

This new type of fireplace design has gained a lot of attention at industry shows and in kitchen and bath magazines. The concept behind this small, vertically-oriented stove is providing a cozy, intimate atmosphere, as might be found in a charming bed and breakfast inn.

The fireplace is designed for corners or limited-space installations in kitchens, bedrooms, or even baths. By elevating the fireplace above the floor, it can be easily seen while seated at a breakfast room table or from a bed.

Bed and breakfast fireplaces come in different styles, such as antique brick and stone. Several choices of face materials are available, including antique gold, brushed nickel, and wrought iron. The fireplaces have fire burners with logs and burn natural or propane gas. Their flues are vented directly to the outdoors, either horizontally or vertically, with an 8" diameter vent.

These fireplaces are available primarily from one manufacturer. *(See the*

"Resources" for more information.) They are heater-rated, with a heating capacity of 650 SF, and provide 16,000 BTUs heat output. The warranty offered depends on the type of fuel used by the insert or fireplace.

This project estimate covers the framing lumber, the firebox and face, the chimney, vent, and gypsum wallboard. The labor includes subcontracted electrical and gasfitter work, including a gas pressure test.

Project Estimate

Description	Quantity	Unit	Labor Hrs Per Unit	Labor Hrs Total	Material Per Unit	Installation Per Unit	Material Total	Installation Total	Total
Self-Performed									
New studs and jacks	96	L.F.	0.01	0.96	0.37	0.59	36	57	93
New wall plates	20	L.F.	0.02	0.40	0.37	0.82	7	16	23
Fireplace support joists	16	L.F.	0.01	0.16	0.37	0.52	6	8	14
Fireplace support deck	10	SF Flr.	0.01	0.10	1.03	0.52	10	5	15
Gypsum wallboard	40	S.F.	0.02	0.80	0.28	0.68	11	27	38
Pre-fabricated firebox	1	Ea.	8	8	1500	325	1,500	325	1,825
Fireplace chimney and vent	3	V.L.F.	0.24	0.72	57	9.90	171	30	201
Electrical minimum	1	Job	4	4		178		178	178
Gasfitter minimum	1	Job	2.67	2.67		118		118	118
Gas pressure test	1	Ea.	3	3		133		133	133
Subtotals							1,741	897	2,638
General Requirements (Site Overhead)						12%	209	108	317
Subtotals							1,950	1,005	2,955
Overhead and Profit						10%	195	101	296
Subtotals							2,145	1,106	3,251

Grand Total $3,251

Photo courtesy of Travis Industries

Cathedral Ceiling

Remove light fixtures, gypsum wallboard, and ceiling joists. Install tie beams, recessed light fixtures, insulation, and gypsum wallboard. Paint.

Raised, cathedral (or "vaulted"), and even domed and coffered ceilings have become popular in kitchen renovations, as homeowners look for ways to add a feeling of spaciousness to older homes that have lower ceilings. This project estimate itemizes the costs to remove a 12' × 16' ceiling above the kitchen in a one-story house with a low-pitch gable roof—and install and then finish a new cathedral ceiling. The estimate assumes that the existing roof is in good condition and weather-tight.

The tasks include disconnecting and taking down a ceiling light fixture and removing the gypsum wallboard ceiling, furring, insulation, ceiling joists, and ridge shingles. The new installation includes tie beams, rafter and soffit vents, furring, insulation, wallboard, lighting circuits, and recessed light fixtures, as well as finishing and painting.

Depending on the exposure and natural light from the kitchen's existing windows, adding skylights to the

cathedral ceiling can be a natural extension to this project. See the "Alternates" box for cost estimates for two skylights, one fixed, and the other operable.

The homeowner might also want to consider adding a ceiling fan (also priced under "Alternates") to save on energy costs and to make the space more comfortable by pushing down warm air in winter, and circulating heat out of the room in summer.

Project Estimate

Description	Quantity	Unit	Labor Hrs Per Unit	Labor Hrs Total	Material Per Unit	Installation Per Unit	Material Total	Installation Total	Total
Self-Performed									
Remove existing ceiling joists	168	L.F.	0.02	3.36		0.49		82	82
Remove debris to dumpster	8	C.Y.	0.97	7.76		28.50		228	228
Install new tie beams	48	L.F.	0.02	0.96	0.59	0.93	28	45	73
Install rafter vents	36	Ea.	0.09	3.24	0.50	3.62	18	130	148
Install soffit vents	32	L.F.	0.04	1.28	0.33	1.63	11	52	63
Remove ridge shingles	1	Job	4	4		150		150	150
Ridge vent	16	L.F.	0.05	0.80	2.34	1.87	37	30	67
Insulation	224	S.F.	0.01	2.24	0.66	0.28	148	63	211
Furring	224	L.F.	0.02	4.48	0.31	0.72	69	161	230
Gypsum wallboard ceiling	224	S.F.	0.02	4.48	0.28	0.85	63	190	253
Paint ceiling	224	S.F.	0.01	2.24	0.16	0.44	36	99	135
Paint tie beams	48	L.F.	0.02	0.96	0.17	0.88	8	42	50
Subcontract									
Disconnect and remove existing light fixture	1	Ea.	0.26	0.26		11.45		11	11
Lighting circuits	4	Ea.	0.32	1.28	10.35	14.20	41	57	98
Recessed lighting	4	Ea.	0.29	1.16	59.50	12.70	238	51	289
Dumpster	1	Week	1	1	375	32.50	375	33	408
Subtotals							1,072	1,424	2,496
General Requirements (Site Overhead)						12%	129	171	300
Subtotals							1,201	1,595	2,796
Overhead and Profit						10%	120	160	280
Subtotals							1,321	1,755	3,076

Grand Total $3,076

Alternates

	Unit	Total Cost
Skylights		
Fixed skylight	Ea.	$315
Flashing for above	Ea.	$101
Ventilating skylight	Ea.	$370
Flashing for above	Ea.	$101
Ceiling Fan		
Lighted variable speed ceiling fan	Ea.	$430
Rough electric for above	Job	$89

New Wall Partition with French Doors

Frame walls. Run wiring for electrical outlets. Apply gypsum wallboard and trim. Install doors. Paint.

Large kitchens are typical in new homes, and remodeling has followed that trend—with homeowners usually wanting to expand their existing kitchen space with additions or use of adjoining areas. However, there are cases where a large space is *too* open, or homeowners want clearly-defined areas—for cooking, entertaining, and doing office work and homework.

This project is one way to reconfigure kitchen and adjoining family or dining room spaces to meet those needs. By adding a partition wall and interior French doors, sound transmission is reduced, and each room can have its own identity and purpose. If the doors and wall will separate the kitchen from the dining room, the dining area becomes more formal, yet still captures some of the kitchen's light, along with visual openness.

Building a new partition is basic remodeling. You'll need to give the homeowner information up-front on the available types and styles of interior French doors, so that this item can be ordered in advance if need be. Considerations like sound transmission, warranties, and architectural style and hardware need to be thought through.

This project estimate includes the materials and labor needed to frame and finish a 10' × 9' wall, with a duplex electrical outlet installed on each side of the door by an electrician. Also covered are new 15-lite interior French doors and the door frame, and final painting of the new walls and ceiling.

Project Estimate

Description	Quantity	Unit	Labor Hrs Per Unit	Labor Hrs Total	Material Per Unit	Installation Per Unit	Material Total	Installation Total	Total
Self-Performed									
New wood framing	10	L.F.	0.16	1.60	3.69	6.50	37	65	102
Gypsum wallboard	160	S.F.	0.02	3.20	0.28	0.68	45	109	154
Interior door frame	20	L.F.	0.04	0.80	6.05	1.74	121	35	156
French doors	2	Ea.	0.89	1.78	233	36	466	72	538
Door trim	40	L.F.	0.03	1.20	0.94	1.36	38	54	92
Baseboard	20	L.F.	0.03	0.60	1.68	1.36	34	27	61
Passage set, non-keyed	2	Ea.	0.67	1.34	45	27	90	54	144
Paint, ceiling and walls, primer	160	S.F.			0.05	0.14	8	22	30
Paint, ceiling and walls, 2 coats	160	S.F.	0.01	1.60	0.11	0.36	18	58	76
Paint trim, including putty, primer	60	L.F.	0.01	0.60	0.03	0.44	2	26	28
Paint trim, including putty, one coat	60	L.F.	0.01	0.60	0.03	0.44	2	26	28
Paint doors, primer and two coats	1	Ea.	4	4	5.75	143	6	143	149
Subcontract									
Duplex receptacles	2	Ea.	0.55	1.10	7.10	24.50	14	49	63
Electrician service charge	1	Day	8	8		355		355	355
Subtotals							881	1,095	1,976
General Requirements (Site Overhead)						12%	106	131	237
Subtotals							987	1,226	2,213
Overhead and Profit						10%	99	123	221
Subtotals							1,086	1,349	2,434

Grand Total   **$2,434**

Door Interference

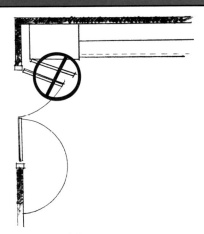

Recommended:
No entry door should interfere with the safe operation of appliances, nor should appliance doors interfere with one another.

Based on guidelines published by the
National Kitchen & Bath Association

Single-Wall Kitchen

Replace flooring, appliances, sink, cabinets, and countertop. Add light fixtures and GFI outlets. Apply molding, trim, and paint.

This project estimate is for a complete kitchen renovation—cabinets and countertops, sink and faucet, appliances, flooring, lighting, and new electrical outlets, as well as wall and ceiling finishes.

As a small room, there is less material to install in a single-wall kitchen, but the scheduling considerations are the same as for a large kitchen. You still need to plan for subcontractors; lead times on the new fixtures, appliances, and materials; and dumpster rental. The restrictions of working in a small space can make precise scheduling even more important, since it may be difficult for more than one task to be performed at the same time.

Single-wall kitchens are the most challenging in terms of creating an efficient layout. The best layout has the sink in the center with 4' of counter space on either side, and the range and refrigerator on or near the ends.

This model estimate includes labor for demolition and removal of the old kitchen components. Among these tasks are replacing the old underlayment to achieve a quality installation of the new hardwood flooring, and removing the old walls and ceiling surfaces. These procedures are done to ensure plumb, level, and smooth surfaces and to simplify installation of new light fixtures and electrical outlets, as well as rough-in

for the new sink. New insulation is also included for the outside wall.

The "Alternates" box lists unit costs for other material choices, including vinyl, laminate, and ceramic and stone tile for the flooring—and laminate, granite, tile, butcher block, and stainless steel for the countertops. The "Alternates" also include costs for a laminate, ceramic tile, and stainless steel backsplash. Different sink and faucet options are listed.

Refer to the flooring, lighting/electrical, and sink/countertop projects for more on those parts of the renovation.

Project Estimate

Description	Quantity	Unit	Labor Hrs Per Unit	Labor Hrs Total	Material Per Unit	Installation Per Unit	Material Total	Installation Total	Total
Self-Performed									
Remove existing dishwasher	1	Ea.	0.80	0.80		23.50		24	24
Remove existing range	1	Ea.	0.73	0.73		21.50		22	22
Remove existing refrigerator	1	Ea.	0.33	0.33		9.80		10	10
Remove existing range hood	1	Ea.	0.67	0.67		19.65		20	20
Remove existing countertop	9	L.F.	0.08	0.72		2.36		21	21
Remove existing base cabinets	6	L.F.	0.20	1.20		5.90		35	35
Remove existing wall cabinets	12	L.F.	0.20	2.40		5.90		71	71
Remove existing ceiling gypsum wallboard	91	S.F.	0.02	1.82		0.59		54	54
Remove existing gypsum wallboard	328	S.F.	0.01	3.28		0.24		79	79
Remove existing insulation	37	C.F.	0.01	0.37		0.17		6	6
Remove existing flooring	65	S.F.	0.02	1.30		0.47		31	31
Remove existing underlayment	65	S.F.	0.01	0.65		0.31		20	20
Debris removal	8	C.Y.	0.67	5.36		19.65		157	157
Insulation at exterior wall	112	S.F.	0.01	1.12	0.30	0.20	34	22	56
Gypsum wallboard ceiling	91	S.F.	0.02	1.82	0.28	0.85	25	77	102
Gypsum wallboard	328	S.F.	0.02	6.56	0.28	0.68	92	223	315
Wall cabinets	3	Ea.	0.70	2.10	232	28.50	696	86	782
Over refrigerator cabinet	1	Ea.	0.65	0.65	198	26.50	198	27	225
Over stove cabinet	1	Ea.	0.70	0.70	189	28.50	189	29	218
Base cabinets	2	Ea.	0.79	1.58	445	32	890	64	954
Sink base cabinet	1	Ea.	0.81	0.81	305	33	305	33	338
Drawer base cabinet	1	Ea.	0.77	0.77	320	31	320	31	351
Solid surface countertop	9	L.F.	0.84	7.56	90.50	34.50	815	311	1,126
Solid surface kitchen sink	1	Ea.	4	4	440	163	440	163	603
Valance board over sink	4	L.F.	0.04	0.16	8.90	1.65	36	7	43
Trim, crown molding, stock pine, 9/16" x 3-5/8"	16	L.F.	0.03	0.48	1.84	1.30	29	21	50
Paint, ceiling & walls, primer	285	S.F.			0.05	0.14	14	40	54
Paint, ceiling & walls, 1 coat	285	S.F.	0.01	2.85	0.05	0.22	14	63	77
Putty and prime cabinet cornice trim	16	L.F.	0.01	0.16	0.03	0.44		7	7
Paint cabinet cornice, 2 coats	16	L.F.	0.01	0.16	0.03	0.44		7	7
Hardwood flooring	65	S.F.	0.05	3.25	3.30	1.92	215	125	340
Sand and finish flooring	65	S.F.	0.03	1.95	0.76	0.80	49	52	101
Cooking range, freestanding, 30" wide, one oven	1	Ea.	1.60	1.60	265	47	265	47	312
Hood for range, 2-speed, 30" wide	1	Ea.	2	2	41	83	41	83	124
Refrigerator, no-frost, 19 C.F.	1	Ea.	2	2	560	59	560	59	619
Dishwasher	1	Ea.	2.50	2.50	272	111	272	111	383
Subcontract									
Remove kitchen sink	1	Ea.	1.14	1.14		50.50		51	51
Kitchen sink faucet	1	Ea.	0.80	0.80	56.50	35.50	57	36	93
Rough-in, supply, waste & vent for sink	1	Ea.	7.48	7.48	115	298	115	298	413
Remove existing light fixture	1	Ea.	0.26	0.26		11.45		11	11
Lighting circuits	3	Ea.	0.25	0.75	4.87	11.10	15	33	48
Recessed lighting fixtures	3	Ea.	0.29	0.87	59.50	12.70	179	38	217
GFI circuits	3	Ea.	0.65	1.95	38.50	29	116	87	203
Dumpster	1	Week	1	1	375	32.50	375	33	408
Subtotals							6,356	2,825	9,181
General Requirements (Site Overhead)						12%	763	339	1,102
Subtotals							7,119	3,164	10,283
Overhead and Profit						10%	712	316	1,028
Subtotals							7,831	3,480	11,311

Grand Total   **$11,311**

Alternates

	Unit	Total Cost
Countertop materials		
Plastic laminate	L.F.	$39
Marble	L.F.	$114
Maple butcher block	L.F.	$80
Granite	L.F.	$147
Ceramic tile	L.F.	$42
Stainless steel	S.F.	$146
Kitchen sinks		
Single bowl porcelain enamel on cast iron	Ea.	$340
Double bowl porcelain enamel on cast iron	Ea.	$450
Single bowl stainless steel	Ea.	$520
Double bowl stainless steel	Ea.	$810
Single bowl enameled steel	Ea.	$235
Double bowl enameled steel	Ea.	$294
Accessories		
Garbage disposal	Ea.	$205
Single control lever handle faucet, with pull-out spray, white	Ea.	$238
Single control lever handle faucet, with pull-out spray, polished chrome	Ea.	$219
Single control lever handle faucet, with pull-out spray, polished brass	Ea.	$256
Backsplash options		
Plastic laminate	S.F.	$6
Ceramic tile	S.F.	$8
Stainless steel	S.F.	$7
Flooring		
Floating laminate flooring	S.F.	$6
Sheet vinyl flooring	S.F.	$5
Linoleum flooring	S.F.	$6
12" x 12" ceramic tile flooring	S.F.	$6
Stone flooring	S.F.	$43

Pro Style

Pot Filler

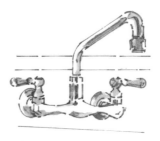

Wall-Mounted

Project Worksheet

	Unit	Quantity	Price per Unit	Total	Dimensions	Source/Model#/ Specs

Galley Kitchen

Replace flooring, cabinets/counters, sink, and appliances, and add new light fixtures and GFI outlets. Install hardwood flooring, apply molding, and paint.

This rectangular space with parallel walls can be one of the most efficient kitchen layouts. With proper distances between them, the cook has easy access to all the elements in the refrigerator/sink/range work triangle.

The drawbacks of the galley kitchen are that traffic has to move directly through the work area if there are doors at both ends of the room, and there is usually no room for an eating area. Typically, the sink and refrigerator are on one wall, with the range on the opposite wall. The floor space in between is usually 4' to 6'.

If a renovation does not allow for expansion through an addition or bump-out, the look, function, and feeling of openness can still be brought up to a whole new level with carefully chosen cabinets, appliances, surface treatments, lighting, and possibly new windows.

One option to open up a galley kitchen and provide a counter/eating area is building an island (or peninsula) on one wall, open to an adjoining breakfast or family room. Glass doors on upper

cabinets are another way to achieve a more spacious look.

This model project estimates the cost to remove the old appliances, cabinets, walls, ceiling, and vinyl sheet flooring, as well as the old light fixture and sink. All of these elements are replaced, with added upgrades to hardwood flooring, solid surface countertops/sink, and crown molding. The "Alternates" box lists costs for other types of flooring, countertops, sinks, faucets, and accessories.

Project Estimate

Description	Quantity	Unit	Labor Hrs Per Unit	Labor Hrs Total	Material Per Unit	Installation Per Unit	Material Total	Installation Total	Total
Self-Performed									
Remove existing dishwasher	1	Ea.	0.80	0.80		23.50		24	24
Remove existing range	1	Ea.	0.73	0.73		21.50		22	22
Remove existing refrigerator	1	Ea.	0.33	0.33		9.80		10	10
Remove existing range hood	1	Ea.	0.67	0.67		19.65		20	20
Remove existing microwave oven	1	Ea.	0.50	0.50		14.75		15	15
Remove existing countertop	18	L.F.	0.08	1.44		2.36		42	42
Remove existing kitchen base cabinets	18	L.F.	0.20	3.60		5.90		106	106
Remove existing kitchen wall cabinets	18	L.F.	0.20	3.60		5.90		106	106
Remove existing gypsum wallboard ceiling	127	S.F.	0.02	2.54		0.59		75	75
Remove existing gypsum wallboard	360	S.F.	0.01	3.60		0.24		86	86
Remove wall insulation	30	C.F.	0.01	0.30		0.17		5	5
Remove existing flooring	96	S.F.	0.02	1.92		0.47		45	45
Remove existing underlayment	127	S.F.	0.01	1.27		0.31		39	39
Remove debris to dumpster	10	C.Y.	0.67	6.70		19.65		197	197
Blocking, for mounting cabinets, 2 x 4	38	L.F.	0.03	1.14	0.37	1.30	14	49	63
Gypsum wallboard	360	S.F.	0.02	7.20	0.28	0.85	101	306	407
Gypsum wallboard ceiling	127	S.F.	0.02	2.54	0.28	0.68	36	86	122
Wall cabinets, 12" deep, 36" wide, 24" high	4	Ea.	0.70	2.80	189	28.50	756	114	870
Over stove cabinet	1	Ea.	0.70	0.70	189	28.50	189	29	218
Over refrigerator cabinet	1	Ea.	0.67	0.67	186	27	186	27	213
Base cabinets, 24" deep, 36" wide	4	Ea.	0.79	3.16	330	32	1,320	128	1,448
Sink base cabinet	1	Ea.	0.81	0.81	305	33	305	33	338
Four drawer cabinet	1	Ea.	0.67	0.67	266	27	266	27	293
Solid surface countertop	18	L.F.	0.84	15.12	71.50	34.50	1,287	621	1,908
Solid surface kitchen sink	1	Ea.	4	4	440	163	440	163	603
Valance board over sink	4	L.F.	0.04	0.16	8.90	1.65	36	7	43
Trim, crown molding, stock pine, 9/16" x 3-5/8"	46	L.F.	0.03	1.38	1.84	1.30	85	60	145
Hardwood flooring	96	S.F.	0.05	4.80	3.30	1.92	317	184	501
Sand and finish hardwood floor	96	S.F.	0.03	2.88	0.76	0.80	73	77	150
Paint, ceiling & walls, primer	425	S.F.			0.05	0.14	21	60	81
Paint, ceiling & walls, 1 coat	425	S.F.	0.01	4.25	0.05	0.22	21	94	115
Paint, cornice trim, simple design, incl. puttying, primer	46	L.F.	0.01	0.46	0.03	0.44	1	20	21
Paint, cornice trim, simple design, one coat	46	L.F.	0.01	0.46	0.03	0.44	1	20	21
Cooking range, freestanding, 30" wide, one oven	1	Ea.	1.60	1.60	265	47	265	47	312
Microwave	1	Ea.	2	2	91	89	91	89	180
Hood for range, 2-speed, 30" wide	1	Ea.	2	2	41	83	41	83	124
Refrigerator, no-frost, 19 C.F.	1	Ea.	2	2	560	59	560	59	619
Dishwasher	1	Ea.	5	5	320	222	320	222	542
Subcontract									
Remove existing kitchen sink	1	Ea.	1.14	1.14		50.50		51	51
Kitchen sink faucet	1	Ea.	0.80	0.80	56.50	35.50	57	36	93
Rough-in, supply, waste & vent for sink	1	Ea.	7.48	7.48	115	298	115	298	413
Remove existing kitchen lighting fixture	1	Ea.	0.26	0.26		11.45		11	11
Lighting circuits	4	Ea.	0.25	1	4.87	11.10	19	44	63
Recessed lighting	4	Ea.	0.29	1.16	59.50	12.70	238	51	289
GFI outlets	4	Ea.	0.65	2.60	38.50	29	154	116	270
Dumpster	2	Week	1	2	365	32.50	730	65	795
Subtotals							8,045	4,069	12,114
General Requirements (Site Overhead)						12%	965	488	1,454
Subtotals							9,010	4,557	13,568
Overhead and Profit						10%	901	456	1,357
Subtotals							9,911	5,013	14,925

Grand Total   **$14,925**

Alternates

Countertop materials	Unit	Total Cost
Plastic laminate	L.F.	$39
Marble	L.F.	$114
Maple butcher block	L.F.	$80
Granite	L.F.	$147
Ceramic tile	L.F.	$42
Stainless steel	S.F.	$146
Kitchen sinks		
Single bowl porcelain enamel on cast iron	Ea.	$340
Double bowl porcelain enamel on cast iron	Ea.	$450
Single bowl stainless steel	Ea.	$520
Double bowl stainless steel	Ea.	$810
Single bowl enameled steel	Ea.	$235
Double bowl enameled steel	Ea.	$294
Accessories		
Garbage disposal	Ea.	$205
Single control lever handle faucet, with pull-out spray, white	Ea.	$238
Single control lever handle faucet, with pull-out spray, polished chrome	Ea.	$219
Single control lever handle faucet, with pull-out spray, polished brass	Ea.	$256
Backsplash options		
Plastic laminate	S.F.	$6
Ceramic tile	S.F.	$8
Stainless steel	S.F.	$7
Flooring		
Floating laminate flooring	S.F.	$6
Sheet vinyl flooring	S.F.	$5
Linoleum flooring	S.F.	$6
12″ x 12″ ceramic tile flooring	S.F.	$6
Stone flooring	S.F.	$43

Backsplashes

- *Usually 18"-24" high.*

- *Should be durable and easy to maintain.*

- *Great place for an accent treatment without a big investment.*

- *Options include:*

  - *Tile: ceramic, stone, glass, or metal, with choice of relief designs.*

  - *Beadboard and V-groove paneling: great for older-style homes. Can also be used on cabinets and appliance fronts to tie in. If staining and sealing, use minimum of 2 coats polyurethane. If painting, use gloss enamel paint.*

  - *Laminate: match or coordinate with counter. Downside is the seam, which is visible and can allow water penetration.*

  - *Solid surface: Usually ½" thick for this use. Can order as integral part of counter to avoid a seam. Can also be separate piece in accent color, routed for decorative effect, or have tiles embedded.*

  - *Metal: options include stainless steel, or for less cost, brushed and sealed aluminum.*

Project Worksheet

	Unit	Quantity	Price per Unit	Total	Dimensions	Source/Model#/ Specs

L-Shaped Kitchen

Remove all components of old kitchen. Install hardwood flooring, cabinets/ countertops, appliances, sink, light fixtures, and GFI outlets. Apply trim and paint.

If the work triangle is set up correctly, this two-sided layout can be very efficient. It's compact, and traffic flows away from the cook, provided the primary counter/work areas are toward the inside of the "L."

An ideal arrangement would be having the refrigerator in an outside corner, the sink in the middle of the same wall, and the range in the middle of the other wall—allowing food preparation to flow in that same order. The dishwasher should be no more than 36" from the sink.

L-shaped kitchens often include islands. If the homeowner's budget is limited, you might want to suggest a two-step plan that allows for a future island unit or peninsula.

The model project estimated here includes removal of all the old appliances, cabinets, and fixtures, and demolition of the flooring, walls, and ceiling.

New surface materials include an upgrade to solid surface countertops and sink, and hardwood flooring. New cabinets and light fixtures are also priced, along with three additional GFI outlets. The economical appliance models help to keep this renovation in reach for many homeowners.

Project Estimate

Description	Quantity	Unit	Labor Hrs Per Unit	Labor Hrs Total	Material Per Unit	Installation Per Unit	Material Total	Installation Total	Total
Self-Performed									
Remove existing dishwasher	1	Ea.	0.80	0.80		23.50		24	24
Remove existing range	1	Ea.	0.73	0.73		21.50		22	22
Remove existing refrigerator	1	Ea.	0.33	0.33		9.80		10	10
Remove existing range hood	1	Ea.	0.67	0.67		19.65		20	20
Remove existing countertop	13	L.F.	0.08	1.04		2.36		31	31
Remove existing base cabinets	12	L.F.	0.20	2.40		5.90		71	71
Remove existing wall cabinets	15	L.F.	0.20	3		5.90		89	89
Remove gypsum wallboard ceiling	96	S.F.	0.02	1.92		0.59		57	57
Remove gypsum wallboard	160	S.F.	0.01	1.60		0.24		38	38
Remove existing flooring	72	S.F.	0.02	1.44		0.47		34	34
Remove existing underlayment	72	S.F.	0.01	0.72		0.31		22	22
Remove existing insulation	96	C.F.	0.01	0.96		0.17		16	16
Remove debris to dumpster	8	C.Y.	0.67	5.36		19.65		157	157
Wall insulation	96	S.F.	0.01	0.96	0.30	0.20	29	19	48
Gypsum wallboard ceiling	96	S.F.	0.02	1.92	0.28	0.85	27	82	109
Gypsum wallboard	1	S.F.	0.02	0.02	0.28	0.68		1	1
Blocking, for mounting cabinets, 2 x 4	32	L.F.	0.03	0.96	0.37	1.30	12	42	54
Wall cabinets, 12" deep, 36" wide, 24" high	5	Ea.	0.70	3.50	232	28.50	1,160	143	1,303
Base cabinets, 24" deep, 36" wide	4	Ea.	0.79	3.16	445	32	1,780	128	1,908
Solid surface countertop	13	L.F.	0.80	10.40	65	32.50	845	423	1,268
Solid surface kitchen sink	1	Ea.	4	4	440	163	440	163	603
Valance board over sink	4	L.F.	0.04	0.16	8.90	1.65	36	7	43
Trim, cornice molding, stock pine, 9/16" x 2-1/4"	20	L.F.	0.03	0.60	0.91	1.09	18	22	40
Hardwood flooring	72	S.F.	0.05	3.60	3.30	1.92	238	138	376
Sand and finish hardwood flooring	72	S.F.	0.03	2.16	0.76	0.80	55	58	113
Paint, ceiling & walls, primer	250	S.F.			0.05	0.14	13	35	48
Paint, ceiling & walls, 1 coat	250	S.F.	0.01	2.50	0.05	0.22	13	55	68
Paint, cornice trim, simple design, incl. putty, primer	20	L.F.	0.01	0.20	0.03	0.44	1	9	10
Paint, cornice trim, simple design, one coat	20	L.F.	0.01	0.20	0.03	0.44	1	9	10
Cooking range, freestanding, 30" wide, one oven	1	Ea.	1.60	1.60	265	47	265	47	312
Hood for range, 2-speed, 30" wide	1	Ea.	2	2	41	83	41	83	124
Refrigerator, no-frost, 19 C.F.	1	Ea.	2	2	560	59	560	59	619
Dishwasher, 2 cycle	1	Ea.	2.50	2.50	272	111	272	111	383
Subcontract									
Remove existing kitchen sink	1	Ea.	1.14	1.14		50.50		51	51
Kitchen faucet	1	Ea.	0.80	0.80	56.50	35.50	57	36	93
Rough-in, supply, waste & vent for sink	1	Ea.	7.48	7.48	115	298	115	298	413
Remove existing lighting	1	Ea.	0.26	0.26		11.45		11	11
Lighting fixture circuits	1	Ea.	0.25	0.25	4.87	11.10	5	11	16
Recessed lighting fixtures	3	Ea.	0.29	0.87	59.50	12.70	179	38	217
GFI outlet circuits	3	Ea.	0.65	1.95	38.50	29	116	87	203
Dumpster	1	Week	1	1	365	32.50	365	33	398
Subtotals							6,643	2,790	9,433
General Requirements (Site Overhead)						12%	797	335	1,132
Subtotals							7,440	3,125	10,565
Overhead and Profit						10%	744	313	1,057
Subtotals							8,184	3,438	11,622

Grand Total   **$11,622**

Alternates

	Unit	Total Cost
Countertop materials		
Plastic laminate	L.F.	$39
Marble	L.F.	$114
Maple butcher block	L.F.	$80
Granite	L.F.	$147
Ceramic tile	L.F.	$42
Stainless steel	S.F.	$146
Kitchen sinks		
Single bowl porcelain enamel on cast iron	Ea.	$340
Double bowl porcelain enamel on cast iron	Ea.	$450
Single bowl stainless steel	Ea.	$520
Double bowl stainless steel	Ea.	$810
Single bowl enameled steel	Ea.	$235
Double bowl enameled steel	Ea.	$294
Accessories		
Garbage disposal	Ea.	$205
Single control lever handle faucet, with pull-out spray, white	Ea.	$238
Single control lever handle faucet, with pull-out spray, polished chrome	Ea.	$219
Single control lever handle faucet, with pull-out spray, polished brass	Ea.	$256
Backsplash options		
Plastic laminate	S.F.	$6
Ceramic tile	S.F.	$8
Stainless steel	S.F.	$7
Flooring		
Floating laminate flooring	S.F.	$6
Sheet vinyl flooring	S.F.	$5
Linoleum flooring	S.F.	$6
12" x 12" ceramic tile flooring	S.F.	$6
Stone flooring	S.F.	$43

Project Worksheet

	Unit	Quantity	Price per Unit	Total	Dimensions	Source/Model#/ Specs

U-ShapedKitchen

> *Gut old kitchen and install hardwood flooring, new cabinets and countertop, sink, appliances, light fixtures, and outlets. Apply trim and paint.*

The U-shaped layout is considered by many designers to be the most efficient. It provides for a lot of cabinets and counter space, and allows two people to work easily at the same time. There should be minimal problems with traffic flow if there are doorways at either end of the open wall. If there is only one entrance to this kitchen, pass-through traffic won't be an issue at all.

Ideally, there should be at least 4' of countertop working area at the wall near the middle of the "U," which requires that the room be a minimum of 8' × 8'. On the other hand, if a U-shaped kitchen is very large, it becomes inefficient, as the refrigerator, sink, and range are too distant from one another. (The key is keeping the total linear feet between these three elements to no more than 26'.) Many U-shaped kitchens have only base cabinets on one side, to open the room to adjoining space.

As with all major renovations, homeowners will have many decisions to make and should start working with a designer or doing their own research well in advance. Specialty items with long lead times need to be specifically identified and committed to, and extras like plumbing and electrical rough-in work (for new fixture/appliance locations) must be clarified and priced in the estimate.

This estimate covers demolition of the old kitchen down to the studs and replacing all surface materials, appliances, lighting, and the sink. The cabinets are mid-range stock. The flooring is upgraded from vinyl sheet to hardwood, and the countertop and sink from laminate to solid surface material. New lighting and five GFI outlets are included. The new appliances are economical models; higher-end units can be substituted.

The "Alternates" box provides costs for different flooring options, including vinyl, laminate, linoleum, and ceramic and stone tile. Countertop options include laminate and granite.

Project Estimate

Description	Quantity	Unit	Labor Hrs Per Unit	Labor Hrs Total	Material Per Unit	Installation Per Unit	Material Total	Installation Total	Total
Self-Performed									
Remove existing dishwasher	1	Ea.	0.80	0.80		23.50		24	24
Remove existing cooking range	1	Ea.	0.73	0.73		21.50		22	22
Remove existing refrigerator	1	Ea.	0.33	0.33		9.80		10	10
Remove existing range hood	1	Ea.	0.67	0.67		19.65		20	20
Remove existing countertop	21	L.F.	0.08	1.68		2.36		50	50
Remove existing base cabinets	15	L.F.	0.20	3		5.90		89	89
Remove existing wall cabinets	21	L.F.	0.20	4.20		5.90		124	124
Remove existing gypsum wallboard ceiling	100	S.F.	0.02	2		0.59		59	59
Remove existing gypsum wallboard	220	S.F.	0.01	2.20		0.24		53	53
Remove existing exterior wall insulation	27	C.F.	0.01	0.27		0.17		5	5
Remove existing flooring	100	S.F.	0.02	2		0.47		47	47
Remove existing underlayment	220	S.F.	0.01	2.20		0.31		68	68
Remove debris to dumpster	14	C.Y.	0.67	9.38		19.65		275	275
Insulation for exterior wall	80	S.F.	0.01	0.80	0.30	0.20	24	16	40
Gypsum wallboard ceiling	100	S.F.	0.02	2	0.28	0.85	28	85	113
Blocking, for mounting cabinets, 2 x 4	50	L.F.	0.03	1.50	0.37	1.30	19	65	84
Gypsum wallboard	220	S.F.	0.02	4.40	0.28	0.68	62	150	212
Wall cabinets, 12" deep, 36" wide	7	Ea.	0.70	4.90	232	28.50	1,624	200	1,824
Base cabinets, 24" deep, 36" wide	5	Ea.	0.79	3.95	445	32	2,225	160	2,385
Solid surface countertop	21	L.F.	0.80	16.80	65	32.50	1,365	683	2,048
Solid surface kitchen sink	1	Ea.	4	4	440	163	440	163	603
Valance board over sink	4	L.F.	0.04	0.16	8.90	1.65	36	7	43
Trim, cornice molding, stock pine, 9/16" x 2-1/4"	30	L.F.	0.03	0.90	0.91	1.09	27	33	60
Paint, ceiling & walls, primer	320	S.F.			0.05	0.14	16	45	61
Paint, ceiling & walls, 1 coat	320	S.F.	0.01	3.20	0.05	0.22	16	70	86
Hardwood flooring	128	S.F.	0.05	6.40	3.30	1.92	422	246	668
Sand and finish flooring	85	S.F.	0.03	2.55	0.76	0.80	65	68	133
Paint, cornice trim, simple design, incl. putty, primer	30	L.F.	0.01	0.30	0.03	0.44	1	13	14
Paint, cornice trim, simple design, one coat	30	L.F.	0.01	0.30	0.03	0.44	1	13	14
Cooking range, freestanding, 30" wide, one oven	1	Ea.	1.60	1.60	265	47	265	47	312
Hood for range, 2-speed, 30" wide	1	Ea.	2	2	41	83	41	83	124
Refrigerator, no-frost, 19 C.F.	1	Ea.	2	2	560	59	560	59	619
Dishwasher, built-in, 2 cycle	1	Ea.	2.50	2.50	272	111	272	111	383
Subcontract									
Remove existing sink & cap pipes	1	Ea.	1.14	1.14		50.50		51	51
Kitchen faucet	1	Ea.	0.80	0.80	56.50	35.50	57	36	93
Rough-in, supply, waste & vent for sink & dishwasher	2	Ea.	7.48	14.96	115	298	230	596	826
Remove existing light fixture and deactivate circuit	1	Ea.	0.26	0.26		11.45		11	11
Undercabinet light, 24" fluorescent strip	4	Ea.	0.33	1.32	58.50	14.80	234	59	293
GFI outlets	5	Ea.	0.65	3.25	38.50	29	193	145	338
Dumpster	2	Week	1	2	365	32.50	730	65	795
Subtotals							8,953	4,126	13,079
General Requirements (Site Overhead)						12%	1,074	495	1,569
Subtotals							10,027	4,621	14,648
Overhead and Profit						10%	1,003	462	1,465
Subtotals							11,030	5,083	16,113

Grand Total   **$16,113**

Alternates

	Unit	Total Cost
Countertop materials		
Plastic laminate	L.F.	$39
Marble	L.F.	$114
Maple butcher block	L.F.	$80
Granite	L.F.	$147
Ceramic tile	L.F.	$42
Stainless steel	S.F.	$146
Kitchen sinks		
Single bowl porcelain enamel on cast iron	Ea.	$340
Double bowl porcelain enamel on cast iron	Ea.	$450
Single bowl stainless steel	Ea.	$520
Double bowl stainless steel	Ea.	$810
Single bowl enameled steel	Ea.	$235
Double bowl enameled steel	Ea.	$294
Accessories		
Garbage disposal	Ea.	$205
Single control lever handle faucet, with pull-out spray, white	Ea.	$238
Single control lever handle faucet, with pull-out spray, polished chrome	Ea.	$219
Single control lever handle faucet, with pull-out spray, polished brass	Ea.	$256
Backsplash options		
Plastic laminate	S.F.	$6
Ceramic tile	S.F.	$8
Stainless steel	S.F.	$7
Flooring		
Floating laminate flooring	S.F.	$6
Sheet vinyl flooring	S.F.	$5
Linoleum flooring	S.F.	$6
12" x 12" ceramic tile flooring	S.F.	$6
Stone flooring	S.F.	$43

Project Worksheet

	Unit	Quantity	Price per Unit	Total	Dimensions	Source/Model#/ Specs

Island Kitchen

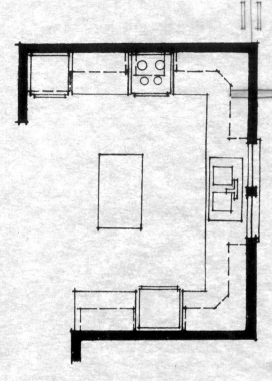

Remove and replace appliances, cabinets, flooring, and wallboard. Add cornice molding and trim, and paint.

This layout refers to any kitchen that comfortably houses an island unit. Island kitchens are often modifications of U- or L-shaped kitchens. Islands lessen the distance from one work center to another and provide additional work or entertaining surfaces. An island can also keep the flow of traffic on the outside of the work area. One situation where an island is not practical is when the main work areas are on opposite walls of the room; the island just ends up getting in the way.

The standard clearance between islands and the counters/cabinets they face is 42" minimum. If your customer has a busy kitchen with two people who like to cook together, 48" would be better.

Very large kitchens may have two islands, one which is more entertainment- or dining-oriented, and another closer to the work triangle for a true work area.

Islands offer several possibilities, depending on their size. Built-in elements might include a cooktop, a sink (for washing vegetables or a specialty model like the new "river" sinks that hold drinks in ice for entertaining), or a butcherblock or stone (e.g., granite or travertine) surface as a visual accent.

Rough-in for the sink is simplified if there's a basement below with access to piping. Don't forget to add the cost of the gas line if there is a gas cooktop or

range planned. Islands should have GFI outlets according to the homeowner's electrical needs.

This project estimate starts with the cost of demolition down to the wall studs and removal of old underlayment, rough-in plumbing for the sink and dishwasher, and electrical work for the new light fixtures and GFIs. The next phase is new walls and ceilings, cabinet and countertop installation (including a desk area), hardwood flooring, and new light fixtures and appliances, along with a coat of paint. The "Alternates" box provides costs for other flooring, countertop, sink, and faucet options.

See the Basic and Deluxe Kitchen Island Unit projects for more detail on islands.

Project Estimate

Description	Quantity		Labor		Cost per Unit		Total Cost		
	Quantity	Unit	Labor Hrs Per Unit	Labor Hrs Total	Material Per Unit	Installation Per Unit	Material Total	Installation Total	Total
Self-Performed									
Remove existing dishwasher	1	Ea.	0.80	0.80		23.50		24	24
Remove existing cooktop	1	Ea.	0.73	0.73		21.50		22	22
Remove existing oven	1	Ea.	0.73	0.73		21.50		22	22
Remove existing refrigerator	1	Ea.	0.33	0.33		9.80		10	10
Remove existing microwave oven	1	Ea.	0.50	0.50		14.75		15	15
Remove existing range hood	1	Ea.	0.67	0.67		19.65		20	20
Remove existing countertop	24	L.F.	0.08	1.92		2.36		57	57
Remove existing base cabinets	30	L.F.	0.20	6		5.90		177	177
Remove existing wall cabinets	27	L.F.	0.20	5.40		5.90		159	159
Remove existing gypsum wallboard ceiling	167	S.F.	0.02	3.34		0.59		99	99
Remove existing gypsum wallboard	416	S.F.	0.01	4.16		0.24		100	100
Remove existing exterior wall insulation	38	C.F.	0.01	0.38		0.17		6	6
Remove existing flooring	125	S.F.	0.02	2.50		0.47		59	59
Remove existing underlayment	125	S.F.	0.01	1.25		0.31		39	39
Remove debris to dumpster	18	C.Y.	0.67	12.06		19.65		354	354
Insulation for exterior wall	116	S.F.	0.01	1.16	0.30	0.20	35	23	58
Gypsum wallboard ceiling	167	S.F.	0.02	3.34	0.28	0.85	47	142	189
Blocking, for mounting cabinets, 2 x 4	68	L.F.	0.03	2.04	0.37	1.30	25	88	113
Gypsum wallboard	416	S.F.	0.02	8.32	0.28	0.68	116	283	399
Wall cabinets, 12" deep, 36" wide	7	Ea.	0.70	4.90	189	28.50	1,323	200	1,523
Range and sink base cabinet	2	Ea.	0.81	1.62	305	33	610	66	676
Tall oven cabinet	1	Ea.	2	2	625	81.50	625	82	707
Base cabinets, 24" deep, 36" wide	6	Ea.	0.79	4.74	330	32	1,980	192	2,172
Over refrigerator cabinet	1	Ea.	0.70	0.70	189	28.50	189	29	218
Corner wall lazy susan cabinet	1	Ea.	1.05	1.05	315	43	315	43	358
Island cabinet	1	Ea.	0.85	0.85	380	34.50	380	35	415
Solid surface countertop	32	L.F.	0.80	25.60	65	32.50	2,080	1,040	3,120
Solid surface kitchen sink	1	Ea.	4	4	440	163	440	163	603
Island solid surface top	4	L.F.	0.80	3.20	65	32.50	260	130	390
Desktop	3	L.F.	0.80	2.40	65	32.50	195	98	293
Shelving at desktop	8	L.F.	0.11	0.88	4.54	4.66	36	37	73
Valance board over sink	4	L.F.	0.04	0.16	8.90	1.65	36	7	43
Trim, cornice molding, stock pine, 9/16" x 2-1/4"	52	L.F.	0.03	1.56	0.91	1.09	47	57	104
Paint, ceiling & walls, primer	590	S.F.			0.05	0.14	30	83	113
Paint, ceiling & walls, 1 coat	590	S.F.	0.01	5.90	0.05	0.22	30	130	160
Hardwood flooring	125	S.F.	0.05	6.25	3.30	1.92	413	240	653
Sand and finish flooring	125	S.F.	0.03	3.75	0.76	0.80	95	100	195
Paint, cornice trim, simple design, incl. puttying, primer	52	L.F.	0.01	0.52	0.03	0.44	2	23	25
Paint, cornice trim, simple design, one coat	52	L.F.	0.01	0.52	0.03	0.44	2	23	25
Wall oven	1	Ea.	2	2	420	89	420	89	509
Hood for cooktop	1	Ea.	2	2	41	83	41	83	124
Refrigerator, no-frost, 19 C.F.	1	Ea.	2	2	560	59	560	59	619
Dishwasher, built-in, 2 cycle	1	Ea.	2.50	2.50	272	111	272	111	383
Microwave oven	1	Ea.	2	2	91	89	91	89	180
Subcontract									
Remove existing sink & cap pipes	1	Ea.	1.14	1.14		50.50		51	51
Kitchen faucet	1	Ea.	0.80	0.80	56.50	35.50	57	36	93
Rough-in, supply, waste & vent for sink & dishwasher	2	Ea.	7.48	14.96	115	298	230	596	826
Remove existing light fixture and deactivate circuit	1	Ea.	0.26	0.26		11.45		11	11
Recessed light fixtures	6	Ea.	0.29	1.74	59.50	12.70	357	76	433
Circuits for light fixtures	6	Ea.	0.25	1.50	4.87	11.10	29	67	96

Project Estimate (cont.)

Description	Quantity		Labor		Cost per Unit		Total Cost		
	Quantity	Unit	Labor Hrs Per Unit	Labor Hrs Total	Material Per Unit	Installation Per Unit	Material Total	Installation Total	Total
Subcontract (cont.)									
Light switches	2	Ea.	0.47	0.94	8.90	21	18	42	60
Undercabinet light, 24" fluorescent strip	4	Ea.	0.33	1.32	58.50	14.80	234	59	293
GFI outlets	5	Ea.	0.65	3.25	38.50	29	193	145	338
Dumpster	2	Week	1	2	365	32.50	730	65	795
Subtotals							12,543	6,056	18,599
General Requirements (Site Overhead)						12%	1,505	727	2,232
Subtotals							14,048	6,783	20,831
Overhead and Profit						10%	1,405	678	2,083
Subtotals							15,453	7,461	22,914

Grand Total   **$22,914**

Alternates

	Unit	Total Cost
Countertop materials		
Plastic laminate	L.F.	$39
Marble	L.F.	$114
Maple butcher block	L.F.	$80
Granite	L.F.	$147
Ceramic tile	L.F.	$42
Stainless steel	S.F.	$146
Kitchen sinks		
Single bowl porcelain enamel on cast iron	Ea.	$340
Double bowl porcelain enamel on cast iron	Ea.	$450
Single bowl stainless steel	Ea.	$520
Double bowl stainless steel	Ea.	$810
Single bowl enameled steel	Ea.	$235
Double bowl enameled steel	Ea.	$294
Accessories		
Garbage disposal	Ea.	$205
Single control lever handle faucet, with pull-out spray, white	Ea.	$238
Single control lever handle faucet, with pull-out spray, polished chrome	Ea.	$219
Single control lever handle faucet, with pull-out spray, polished brass	Ea.	$256
Backsplash options		
Plastic laminate	S.F.	$6
Ceramic tile	S.F.	$8
Stainless steel	S.F.	$7
Flooring		
Floating laminate flooring	S.F.	$6
Sheet vinyl flooring	S.F.	$5
Linoleum flooring	S.F.	$6
12" x 12" ceramic tile flooring	S.F.	$6
Stone flooring	S.F.	$43

Project Worksheet

	Unit	Quantity	Price per Unit	Total	Dimensions	Source/Model#/ Specs

Accessible Kitchen

Remove all elements of old kitchen. Install new cabinets, non-slip tile flooring, appliances, light fixtures, and outlets. Trim and paint.

The terms *universal* and *accessible* are sometimes used interchangeably, but in fact, each has its own meaning. *Universal* (sometimes called *ergonomic*) design refers to adaptations that allow people to interact with a space comfortably. For kitchens, this would include things like custom countertop and cabinet heights, and convenient storage systems that cause the least strain in taking out and putting away large or heavy items.

Accessible design, on the other hand, is geared specifically to wheelchair users, although it can be helpful to anyone with restricted mobility—a growing percentage of our aging population.

Before starting this complete kitchen renovation, consult standards such as the Americans with Disabilities Act and those developed by the American National Standards Institute (ANSI) and the National Kitchen and Bath Association (NKBA) for specifics. *(See the "Resources" at the back of this book for contact information.)* Some basic requirements/recommendations:

- At least 30" × 48" of clear floor space for a front or parallel approach to appliances, countertops, etc.
- 5' of floor space between cabinets on opposing walls.

- Countertops and sinks no more than 34" above the finished floor. Ideally, the sink and range should be 30"-32" and the working counter (e.g., for an electric mixer or other small appliances) should be 27".
- 24" minimum height for knee clearance.
- 24" minimum width for knee clearance.
- 52"-60" reach to high shelves.
- Accessible controls and handles, including stove knobs and faucet controls, at or toward the front.
- Slip-resistant flooring.
- Lever, loop, or other easily manipulated handles.

Project Estimate

Description	Quantity		Labor		Cost per Unit		Total Cost		
	Quantity	Unit	Labor Hrs Per Unit	Labor Hrs Total	Material Per Unit	Installation Per Unit	Material Total	Installation Total	Total
Self-Performed									
Remove existing range	1	Ea.	0.73	0.73		21.50		22	22
Remove existing refrigerator	1	Ea.	0.33	0.33		9.80		10	10
Remove existing range hood	1	Ea.	0.67	0.67		19.65		20	20
Remove existing countertop	9	L.F.	0.08	0.72		2.36		21	21
Remove existing base cabinets	6	L.F.	0.20	1.20		5.90		35	35
Remove existing wall cabinets	12	L.F.	0.20	2.40		5.90		71	71
Remove gypsum wallboard ceiling in existing kitchen	91	S.F.	0.02	1.82		0.59		54	54
Remove gypsum wallboard in existing kitchen and on partition	440	S.F.	0.01	4.40		0.24		106	106
Remove exterior wall insulation	37	C.F.	0.01	0.37		0.17		6	6
Remove flooring	91	S.F.	0.02	1.82		0.47		43	43
Remove underlayment	91	S.F.	0.01	0.91		0.31		28	28
Remove partition framing	112	S.F.	0.01	1.12		0.39		44	44
Remove debris	10	C.Y.	0.67	6.70		19.65		197	197
Exterior wall insulation	112	S.F.	0.01	1.12	0.30	0.20	34	22	56
Gypsum wallboard ceiling with patching to existing	94	S.F.	0.02	1.88	0.28	0.85	26	80	106
Blocking, for mounting cabinets, 2 x 4	18	L.F.	0.03	0.54	0.37	1.30	7	23	30
Gypsum wallboard	220	S.F.	0.02	4.40	0.28	0.68	62	150	212
Wall cabinets	3	Ea.	0.83	2.49	234	34	702	102	804
Pantry style cabinets	3	Ea.	1.60	4.80	430	65	1,290	195	1,485
Base cabinet	1	Ea.	0.79	0.79	330	32	330	32	362
Base cabinet with drawers	1	Ea.	0.72	0.72	320	29	320	29	349
Over stove cabinet	1	Ea.	0.70	0.70	189	28.50	189	29	218
Over refrigerator cabinet	1	Ea.	0.67	0.67	186	27	186	27	213
Solid surface countertop	9	L.F.	0.80	7.20	65	32.50	585	293	878
Trim, crown molding, stock pine, 9/16" x 3-5/8"	28	L.F.	0.03	0.84	1.84	1.30	52	36	88
Paint, ceiling & walls, primer	314	S.F.			0.05	0.14	16	44	60
Paint, ceiling & walls, 1 coat	314	S.F.	0.01	3.14	0.05	0.22	16	69	85
Paint, cornice trim, simple design, incl. puttying, primer	28	L.F.	0.01	0.28	0.03	0.44	1	12	13
Paint, cornice trim, simple design, 1 coat	28	L.F.	0.01	0.28	0.03	0.44	1	12	13
Cooking range, freestanding, 30" wide, one oven	1	Ea.	1.60	1.60	265	47	265	47	312
Hood for range, 2-speed, 30" wide	1	Ea.	2	2	41	83	41	83	124
Refrigerator, no-frost, side-by-side	1	Ea.	5.33	5.33	2275	157	2,275	157	2,432
Cementitious backerboard for quarry tile floors	65	S.F.	0.03	1.95	1.15	1.24	75	81	156
Non-slip quarry tiles	65	S.F.	0.11	7.15	3.29	3.74	214	243	457
Subcontract									
Remove existing sink	1	Ea.	1.14	1.14		50.50		51	51
Kitchen sink faucet	1	Ea.	0.80	0.80	56.50	35.50	57	36	93
Rough-in, supply, waste & vent for sink	1	Ea.	7.48	7.48	115	298	115	298	413
Remove existing light fixture	1	Ea.	0.26	0.26		11.45		11	11
Lighting circuits	4	Ea.	0.25	1	4.87	11.10	19	44	63
Recessed lighting	4	Ea.	0.29	1.16	59.50	12.70	238	51	289
GFI circuits	4	Ea.	0.65	2.60	38.50	29	154	116	270
Dumpster	1	Week	1	1	375	32.50	375	33	408
Subtotals							7,645	3,063	10,708
General Requirements (Site Overhead)						12%	917	368	1,285
Subtotals							8,562	3,431	11,993
Overhead and Profit						10%	856	343	1,199
Subtotals							9,418	3,774	13,192

Grand Total   **$13,192**

If you're assisting with the design, you might want to suggest features like pull-out drawers and shelves and lazy susans, along with appliance garages that can store items within easy reach. Side-by-side or freezer-on-the-bottom refrigerators and staggered stove burners (to prevent reaching over a hot surface) are also a good idea. Dishwashers can be elevated off the floor, possibly within cabinets designed to house wall ovens.

If low vision is a problem for the home's resident, high levels of task lighting (positioned to avoid shadows) and light, non-reflective surfaces with good contrast will be needed.

This project estimate covers removal of existing kitchen walls and flooring, including framing (to enlarge the available space), as well as the old appliances, cabinets, and countertop. The new kitchen includes cabinets configured for wheelchair access, non-slip flooring, new GFI outlets and lighting (with accessible switches), appliances, and a sink with lever handles.

Alternates

	Unit	Total Cost
Countertop materials		
Plastic laminate	L.F.	$39
Marble	L.F.	$114
Maple butcher block	L.F.	$80
Granite	L.F.	$147
Ceramic tile	L.F.	$42
Stainless steel	S.F.	$146
Kitchen sinks		
Single bowl porcelain enamel on cast iron	Ea.	$340
Double bowl porcelain enamel on cast iron	Ea.	$450
Single bowl stainless steel	Ea.	$520
Double bowl stainless steel	Ea.	$810
Single bowl enameled steel	Ea.	$235
Double bowl enameled steel	Ea.	$294
Accessories		
Garbage disposal	Ea.	$205
Single control lever handle faucet, with pull-out spray, white	Ea.	$238
Single control lever handle faucet, with pull-out spray, polished chrome	Ea.	$219
Single control lever handle faucet, with pull-out spray, polished brass	Ea.	$256
Backsplash options		
Plastic laminate	S.F.	$6
Ceramic tile	S.F.	$8
Stainless steel	S.F.	$7
Flooring		
Floating laminate flooring	S.F.	$6
Sheet vinyl flooring	S.F.	$5
Linoleum flooring	S.F.	$6
12" x 12" ceramic tile flooring	S.F.	$6
Stone flooring	S.F.	$43

Project Worksheet

	Unit	Quantity	Price per Unit	Total	Dimensions	Source/Model#/ Specs

Large Kitchen/Family Room with Laundry

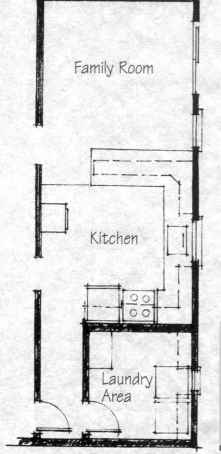

Family Room

Kitchen

Laundry Area

Gut old kitchen and adjacent area, and partition the new space. Install hardwood and tile flooring, cabinets/countertop, sink, appliances, light fixtures, outlets, and dryer connection. Apply molding. Paint and finish.

In new homes, the kitchen/family room area is recognized as the focal point of the household, with a larger space, more decorative details, and a strong emphasis on function and amenities. Fortunately, the small kitchens of older homes can often be opened up to an adjoining breakfast room, formal dining room, porch, or other space—and brightened with new windows or skylights.

This kitchen project has extra features to plan for—the finishes and lighting in the family room, and the features of the separate laundry room, which has its own storage cabinets, appliances, and finishes. The laundry also requires supply and drain pipes, vent pipes, and

dryer ventilation. If the washer (and possibly sink) will be near an existing drain, vertical runs of pipe, or a chase, you can tap into those lines.

In addition to the kitchen appliance power requirements, a 240-volt circuit is needed for the electric clothes dryer, or possibly some re-piping if a gas dryer is required. If the service panel can accommodate it, wiring should be pretty straightforward, especially in a total remodel like this one where the walls and ceiling are removed and replaced.

Another consideration for the laundry room is noise reduction. Even with newer, quieter appliances, it's a good idea to provide sound-proofing fiberglass or foam board insulation. If

there's room for a 2' × 6' wall, you can maximize the insulation.

The project estimated here is a tear-out of an existing kitchen down to the studs, and installation of a new kitchen/family room with a separate laundry. The electrical work includes wiring and installation of four recessed lights, a 240-volt dryer connection, and four GFI outlets. Plumbing involves removal of the old sink/faucet, and rough-in for the new sink/faucet and washing machine. New insulation and gypsum wallboard, trim, painting, flooring, cabinets, a solid surface countertop/sink, and appliances round out the job. The laundry room flooring is cementitious backerboard underneath ceramic tile; the kitchen flooring is hardwood.

Project Estimate

Description	Quantity		Labor		Cost per Unit		Total Cost		
	Quantity	Unit	Labor Hrs Per Unit	Labor Hrs Total	Material Per Unit	Installation Per Unit	Material Total	Installation Total	Total
Self-Performed									
Remove existing dishwasher	1	Ea.	0.80	0.80		23.50		24	24
Remove existing range	1	Ea.	0.73	0.73		21.50		22	22
Remove existing refrigerator	1	Ea.	0.33	0.33		9.80		10	10
Remove existing range hood	1	Ea.	0.67	0.67		19.65		20	20
Remove existing countertop	13	L.F.	0.08	1.04		2.36		31	31
Remove existing base cabinets	12	L.F.	0.20	2.40		5.90		71	71
Remove existing wall cabinets	15	L.F.	0.20	3		5.90		89	89
Remove gypsum wallboard ceiling	420	S.F.	0.02	8.40		0.59		248	248
Remove gypsum wallboard	880	S.F.	0.01	8.80		0.24		211	211
Remove existing flooring	228	S.F.	0.02	4.56		0.47		107	107
Remove existing underlayment	228	S.F.	0.01	2.28		0.31		71	71
Remove existing insulation	135	C.F.	0.01	1.35		0.17		23	23
Remove debris to dumpster	16	C.Y.	0.67	10.72		19.65		314	314
Wall insulation	408	S.F.	0.01	4.08	0.30	0.20	122	82	204
Gypsum wallboard ceiling	420	S.F.	0.02	8.40	0.28	0.85	118	357	475
Gypsum wallboard	880	S.F.	0.02	17.60	0.28	0.68	246	598	844
Blocking, for mounting cabinets, 2 x 4	32	L.F.	0.03	0.96	0.37	1.30	12	42	54
Corner wall cabinet	1	Ea.	0.89	0.89	257	36	257	36	293
Oven cabinet	1	Ea.	2	2	945	81.50	945	82	1,027
Wall cabinets	2	Ea.	0.70	1.40	232	28.50	464	57	521
Wall cabinets	3	Ea.	0.83	2.49	234	34	702	102	804
Over refrigerator cabinet	1	Ea.	0.67	0.67	186	27	186	27	213
Over stove cabinet	1	Ea.	0.70	0.70	189	28.50	189	29	218
Refrigerator enclosure panels	2	Ea.	1.14	2.28	84	46.50	168	93	261
Base cabinets	5	Ea.	0.79	3.95	445	32	2,225	160	2,385
Sink front cabinet	1	Ea.	0.79	0.79	285	32	285	32	317
Corner base cabinet	1	Ea.	0.89	0.89	420	36	420	36	456
Laundry cabinets	2	Ea.	1.60	3.20	570	65	1,140	130	1,270
Laundry shelving	36	L.F.	0.11	3.96	4.54	4.66	163	168	331
Solid surface countertop	24	L.F.	1.07	25.68	112	43.50	2,688	1,044	3,732
Solid surface kitchen sink	1	Ea.	4	4	440	163	440	163	603
Valance board over sink	4	L.F.	0.04	0.16	8.90	1.65	36	7	43
Trim, cornice molding, stock pine, 9/16" x 2-1/4"	20	L.F.	0.03	0.60	0.91	1.09	18	22	40
Cementitious backerboard for laundry floor underlayment	72	S.F.	0.03	2.16	1.15	1.24	83	89	172
Ceramic tile base for laundry room	34	L.F.	0.18	6.12	3.43	5.75	117	196	313
Ceramic tile floor for laundry	72	S.F.	0.07	5.04	3.51	2.33	253	168	421
Hardwood flooring	120	S.F.	0.05	6	3.30	1.92	396	230	626
Sand and finish new and existing hardwood flooring	312	S.F.	0.03	9.36	0.76	0.80	237	250	487
Paint, ceiling & walls, primer	1300	S.F.			0.05	0.14	65	182	247
Paint, ceiling & walls, 1 coat	1300	S.F.	0.01	13	0.05	0.22	65	286	351
Paint, cornice trim, simple design, incl. puttying, primer	20	L.F.	0.01	0.20	0.03	0.44	1	9	10
Paint, cornice trim, simple design, one coat	20	L.F.	0.01	0.20	0.03	0.44	1	9	10
Wall ovens	2	Ea.	4	8	3300	178	6,600	356	6,956
Cooktop	1	Ea.	4	4	1750	178	1,750	178	1,928
Microwave oven	1	Ea.	2	2	550	89	550	89	639
Hood for range, 2-speed, 30" wide	1	Ea.	4	4	1050	166	1,050	166	1,216
Refrigerator, no-frost, 19 C.F.	1	Ea.	5.33	5.33	6325	157	6,325	157	6,482
Dishwasher, 2 cycle	1	Ea.	3.33	3.33	296	148	296	148	444
New washing machine	1	Ea.	2.67	2.67	305	118	305	118	423
New dryer	1	Ea.	5.33	5.33	310	188	310	188	498

Project Estimate (cont.)

Description	Quantity		Labor		Cost per Unit		Total Cost		
	Quantity	Unit	Labor Hrs Per Unit	Labor Hrs Total	Material Per Unit	Installation Per Unit	Material Total	Installation Total	Total
Subcontract (cont.)									
Remove existing kitchen sink	1	Ea.	1.14	1.14		50.50		51	51
Kitchen faucet	1	Ea.	0.80	0.80	56.50	35.50	57	36	93
Rough-in, supply, waste & vent for sink	1	Ea.	7.48	7.48	115	298	115	298	413
Laundry rough-in	1	Ea.	7.48	7.48	115	298	115	298	413
Remove existing lighting	2	Ea.	0.26	0.52		11.45		23	23
Lighting fixture circuits	4	Ea.	0.25	1	4.87	11.10	19	44	63
Recessed lighting fixtures	6	Ea.	0.29	1.74	59.50	12.70	357	76	433
GFI outlet circuits	4	Ea.	0.65	2.60	38.50	29	154	116	270
Dryer electrical connection	1	Ea.	1.25	1.25	59.50	55.50	60	56	116
Dumpster	1	Week	1	1	365	32.50	365	33	398
Subtotals							30,470	8,358	38,828
General Requirements (Site Overhead)						12%	3,656	1,003	4,659
Subtotals							34,126	9,361	43,487
Overhead and Profit						10%	3,413	936	4,349
Subtotals							37,539	10,297	47,836

Grand Total   **$47,836**

Alternates

	Unit	Total Cost
Countertop materials		
Plastic laminate	L.F.	$39
Marble	L.F.	$114
Maple butcher block	L.F.	$80
Granite	L.F.	$147
Ceramic tile	L.F.	$42
Stainless steel	S.F.	$146
Kitchen sinks		
Single bowl porcelain enamel on cast iron	Ea.	$340
Double bowl porcelain enamel on cast iron	Ea.	$450
Single bowl stainless steel	Ea.	$520
Double bowl stainless steel	Ea.	$810
Single bowl enameled steel	Ea.	$235
Double bowl enameled steel	Ea.	$294
Accessories		
Garbage disposal	Ea.	$205
Single control lever handle faucet, with pull-out spray, white	Ea.	$238
Single control lever handle faucet, with pull-out spray, polished chrome	Ea.	$219
Single control lever handle faucet, with pull-out spray, polished brass	Ea.	$256
Backsplash options		
Plastic laminate	S.F.	$6
Ceramic tile	S.F.	$8
Stainless steel	S.F.	$7
Flooring		
Floating laminate flooring	S.F.	$6
Sheet vinyl flooring	S.F.	$5
Linoleum flooring	S.F.	$6
12″ x 12″ ceramic tile flooring	S.F.	$6
Stone flooring	S.F.	$43

Some Faucet Options

Gooseneck

Pullout and Pulldown

Conventional

Project Worksheet

	Unit	Quantity	Price per Unit	Total	Dimensions	Source/Model#/ Specs

Large Kitchen/Family Room with Mudroom

Mudroom

Kitchen

Family Room

Remove all old kitchen components. Partition the new space. Install hardwood and tile flooring, cabinets/countertops, appliances, sink, and light fixtures. Apply trim and paint.

Remodeling the kitchen and family room at the same time, and taking the walls down to the studs, allows for redistribution of the space and can be a good opportunity to incorporate a mudroom. This is a major project, involving complete refinishing of the family room area, a whole new kitchen, and partitioning and finishing the mudroom.

Basic mudroom features include storage, lighting, and a source of heat. Here are some additional mudroom ideas:

• A closet with shelves, a rod, hooks, cubbies, or whatever features are most useful to the homeowner.

• Kitchen- or pantry-type cabinets on one wall—with shelves, hooks, and space to hang coats and jackets. If the room is small, a 10" deep built-in cupboard can hold hooks for coats

and jackets. The cupboard should be at least 60" high with enough space inside for boots and shoes. If the room can accommodate deeper cupboards, you could add options like pull-out shelves and bins for recycling, pet food, sports equipment, or other items.

• Hooks on one wall, installed using a 1' × 4' (or decorative board selected by the homeowner) attached to the studs. If there are small children in the house, include low hooks. Locate all hooks out of the line of traffic.

• A durable, easy-to-clean floor material, such as ceramic tile or resilient flooring.

• A source of heat in the mudroom helps to dry wet outerwear.

• A couple of electrical outlets—to service a lamp or provide an out-of-the-way place to charge cell phones.

• A mirror near the door. A shelf below is a nice option.

Also, find out if the homeowner would like to include any furniture, such as a bench or chest of drawers. If they have a specific piece in mind, ask where it will be placed and measure it to make sure it will fit as planned in the finished space.

The model project estimated here involves tearing out an existing kitchen, including all the old appliances, fixtures, cabinets, and finished floor and walls. New cabinets, a solid surface countertop and sink, new underlayment and hardwood flooring, walls, appliances and recessed light fixtures are part of the renovation.

Costs are included for wiring for the lighting and GFI outlets, and plumbing for the replacement sink. The mudroom requires framing partition walls and a closet, and a ceramic tile floor.

Project Estimate

Description	Quantity		Labor		Cost per Unit		Total Cost		
	Quantity	Unit	Labor Hrs Per Unit	Labor Hrs Total	Material Per Unit	Installation Per Unit	Material Total	Installation Total	Total
Self-Performed									
Remove existing dishwasher	1	Ea.	0.80	0.80		23.50		24	24
Remove existing range	1	Ea.	0.73	0.73		21.50		22	22
Remove existing refrigerator	1	Ea.	0.33	0.33		9.80		10	10
Remove existing range hood	1	Ea.	0.67	0.67		19.65		20	20
Remove existing countertop	13	L.F.	0.08	1.04		2.36		31	31
Remove existing base cabinets	12	L.F.	0.20	2.40		5.90		71	71
Remove existing wall cabinets	15	L.F.	0.20	3		5.90		89	89
Remove gypsum wallboard ceiling	420	S.F.	0.02	8.40		0.59		248	248
Remove gypsum wallboard	880	S.F.	0.01	8.80		0.24		211	211
Remove existing flooring	228	S.F.	0.02	4.56		0.47		107	107
Remove existing underlayment	228	S.F.	0.01	2.28		0.31		71	71
Remove existing insulation	135	C.F.	0.01	1.35		0.17		23	23
Remove debris to dumpster	16	C.Y.	0.67	10.72		19.65		314	314
Wall insulation	408	S.F.	0.01	4.08	0.30	0.20	122	82	204
Gypsum wallboard ceiling	420	S.F.	0.02	8.40	0.28	0.85	118	357	475
Gypsum wallboard	1008	S.F.	0.02	20.16	0.28	0.68	282	685	967
Blocking, for mounting cabinets, 2 x 4	32	L.F.	0.03	0.96	0.37	1.30	12	42	54
Closet framing	8	L.F.	0.16	1.28	3.69	6.50	30	52	82
Corner wall cabinet	1	Ea.	0.89	0.89	257	36	257	36	293
Oven cabinet	1	Ea.	2	2	945	81.50	945	82	1,027
Wall cabinets	2	Ea.	0.70	1.40	232	28.50	464	57	521
Wall cabinets	3	Ea.	0.83	2.49	234	34	702	102	804
Over refrigerator cabinet	1	Ea.	0.67	0.67	186	27	186	27	213
Over stove cabinet	1	Ea.	0.70	0.70	189	28.50	189	29	218
Refrigerator enclosure panels	2	Ea.	1.14	2.28	84	46.50	168	93	261
Base cabinets	5	Ea.	0.79	3.95	445	32	2,225	160	2,385
Sink front cabinet	1	Ea.	0.79	0.79	285	32	285	32	317
Corner base cabinet	1	Ea.	0.89	0.89	420	36	420	36	456
Solid surface countertop	24	L.F.	1.07	25.68	112	43.50	2,688	1,044	3,732
Solid surface kitchen sink	1	Ea.	4	4	440	163	440	163	603
Valance board over sink	4	L.F.	0.04	0.16	8.90	1.65	36	7	43
Bi-fold door frame	20	L.F.	0.04	0.80	6.05	1.74	121	35	156
Bi-fold door trim	40	L.F.	0.03	1.20	0.94	1.36	38	54	92
Closet shelf and pole	1	Ea.	0.53	0.53	23	21.50	23	22	45
Paint bi-fold doors	2	Ea.	2.67	5.34	6.50	95.50	13	191	204
Bi-fold closet doors	1	Ea.	1.60	1.60	310	65	310	65	375
Trim, cornice molding, stock pine, 9/16" x 2-1/4"	20	L.F.	0.03	0.60	0.91	1.09	18	22	40
Cementitious backerboard for mudroom floor underlayment	72	S.F.	0.03	2.16	1.15	1.24	83	89	172
Ceramic tile base for mudroom room	34	L.F.	0.18	6.12	3.43	5.75	117	196	313
Ceramic tile floor for mudroom	72	S.F.	0.07	5.04	3.51	2.33	253	168	421
Hardwood flooring	120	S.F.	0.05	6	3.30	1.92	396	230	626
Sand and finish new and existing hardwood flooring	312	S.F.	0.03	9.36	0.76	0.80	237	250	487
Paint, ceiling & walls, primer	1428	S.F.			0.05	0.14	71	200	271
Paint, ceiling & walls, 1 coat	1428	S.F.	0.01	14.28	0.05	0.22	71	314	385
Paint, cornice trim, simple design, incl. puttying, primer	20	L.F.	0.01	0.20	0.03	0.44	1	9	10
Paint, cornice trim, simple design, one coat	20	L.F.	0.01	0.20	0.03	0.44	1	9	10
Wall ovens	2	Ea.	4	8	3300	178	6,600	356	6,956
Cooktop	1	Ea.	4	4	1750	178	1,750	178	1,928
Microwave oven	1	Ea.	2	2	550	89	550	89	639
Hood for range, 2-speed, 30" wide	1	Ea.	4	4	1050	166	1,050	166	1,216
Refrigerator, no-frost, 19 C.F.	1	Ea.	5.33	5.33	6325	157	6,325	157	6,482
Dishwasher, 2 cycle	1	Ea.	3.33	3.33	296	148	296	148	444

Project Estimate (cont.)

Description	Quantity		Labor		Cost per Unit		Total Cost		
	Quantity	Unit	Labor Hrs Per Unit	Labor Hrs Total	Material Per Unit	Installation Per Unit	Material Total	Installation Total	Total
Subcontract									
Remove existing kitchen sink	1	Ea.	1.14	1.14		50.50		51	51
Kitchen faucet	1	Ea.	0.80	0.80	56.50	35.50	57	36	93
Rough-in, supply, waste & vent for sink	1	Ea.	7.48	7.48	115	298	115	298	413
Remove existing lighting	2	Ea.	0.26	0.52		11.45		23	23
Lighting fixture circuits	4	Ea.	0.25	1	4.87	11.10	19	44	63
Recessed lighting fixtures	6	Ea.	0.29	1.74	59.50	12.70	357	76	433
GFI outlet circuits	4	Ea.	0.65	2.60	38.50	29	154	116	270
Dumpster	1	Week	1	1	365	32.50	365	33	398
Subtotals							28,960	7,952	36,912
General Requirements (Site Overhead)						12%	3,475	954	4,429
Subtotals							32,435	8,906	41,341
Overhead and Profit						10%	3,244	891	4,134
Subtotals							35,679	9,797	45,475

Grand Total $45,475

Alternates

	Unit	Total Cost
Countertop materials		
Plastic laminate	L.F.	$39
Marble	L.F.	$114
Maple butcher block	L.F.	$80
Granite	L.F.	$147
Ceramic tile	L.F.	$42
Stainless steel	S.F.	$146
Kitchen sinks		
Single bowl porcelain enamel on cast iron	Ea.	$340
Double bowl porcelain enamel on cast iron	Ea.	$450
Single bowl stainless steel	Ea.	$520
Double bowl stainless steel	Ea.	$810
Single bowl enameled steel	Ea.	$235
Double bowl enameled steel	Ea.	$294
Accessories		
Garbage disposal	Ea.	$205
Single control lever handle faucet, with pull-out spray, white	Ea.	$238
Single control lever handle faucet, with pull-out spray, polished chrome	Ea.	$219
Single control lever handle faucet, with pull-out spray, polished brass	Ea.	$256
Backsplash options		
Plastic laminate	S.F.	$6
Ceramic tile	S.F.	$8
Stainless steel	S.F.	$7
Flooring		
Floating laminate flooring	S.F.	$6
Sheet vinyl flooring	S.F.	$5
Linoleum flooring	S.F.	$6
12" x 12" ceramic tile flooring	S.F.	$6
Stone flooring	S.F.	$43

Project Worksheet

	Unit	Quantity	Price per Unit	Total	Dimensions	Source/Model#/ Specs

Standard Kitchen with Pantry

Kitchen

Pantry

Demolish the old kitchen. Install wallboard, trim/molding, hardwood flooring, cabinets/countertops, appliances, sink, and light fixtures/outlets. Hang pantry door and install shelving.

Pantries, once a common feature in homes of a certain size, are making a comeback, as new homebuilders, especially of higher-end houses, try to accommodate buyers' growing desire for storage and convenience. A "butler's pantry" usually refers to an area that is separate from, but linked to the kitchen—with matching countertops, cabinets, and possibly a bar sink. A smaller closet-type pantry, such as the one estimated as part of this kitchen renovation, can be constructed like any closet, or made up of one or more cabinets.

While there's no question that this whole kitchen renovation is a major project, the appliances and cabinets in this estimate are "standard" (modestly priced), which brings the overall cost

within more homeowners' budgets. Replacing the appliances allows for a uniform style/finish and some new convenience and energy-saving features, even in many lower-priced models.

This estimate includes a bit of a splurge for solid surface countertop/sink, and hardwood flooring. It also includes under-cabinet lighting, a nice touch at a relatively low cost.

Gutting the kitchen and starting over from scratch gives the homeowner the option to dramatically change the layout to improve the work triangle and traffic flow. Selecting materials and appliances and deciding on a final layout can take several months for busy homeowners. You'll need to give your clients some deadlines to keep the overall project on track.

Be sure to clarify extra costs associated with new rough-in work when fixtures and appliances are moved to new locations. You'll also need to get clarification on any specialty pantry storage items—such as drawers, bins, sliding shelves, cubbies, wine racks, tray slots, or peg boards.

This project estimate is for a complete kitchen renovation that includes not only removing and replacing all the old cabinets, countertops, flooring, sink, and appliances, but also gutting and replacing the walls and ceiling, and building in a new pantry with shelving.

The "Alternates" box includes costs for various other flooring, countertop, sink, and faucet materials. Refer to the other project estimates for more detail on individual kitchen components.

Project Estimate

Description	Quantity		Labor		Cost per Unit		Total Cost		
	Quantity	Unit	Labor Hrs Per Unit	Labor Hrs Total	Material Per Unit	Installation Per Unit	Material Total	Installation Total	Total
Self-Performed									
Remove existing dishwasher	1	Ea.	0.80	0.80		23.50		24	24
Remove existing cooking range	1	Ea.	0.73	0.73		21.50		22	22
Remove existing refrigerator	1	Ea.	0.33	0.33		9.80		10	10
Remove existing range hood	1	Ea.	0.67	0.67		19.65		20	20
Remove existing countertop	21	L.F.	0.08	1.68		2.36		50	50
Remove existing base cabinets	15	L.F.	0.20	3		5.90		89	89
Remove existing wall cabinets	21	L.F.	0.20	4.20		5.90		124	124
Remove existing gypsum wallboard ceiling	50	S.F.	0.02	1		0.59		30	30
Remove existing gypsum wallboard	50	S.F.	0.01	0.50		0.24		12	12
Remove existing exterior wall insulation	27	C.F.	0.01	0.27		0.17		5	5
Remove existing flooring	100	S.F.	0.02	2		0.47		47	47
Remove existing underlayment	220	S.F.	0.01	2.20		0.31		68	68
Remove debris to dumpster	14	C.Y.	0.67	9.38		19.65		275	275
Insulation for exterior wall	80	S.F.	0.01	0.80	0.30	0.20	24	16	40
Gypsum wallboard ceiling	100	S.F.	0.02	2	0.28	0.85	28	85	113
Blocking, for mounting cabinets, 2 x 4	50	L.F.	0.03	1.50	0.37	1.30	19	65	84
Gypsum wallboard	220	S.F.	0.02	4.40	0.28	0.68	62	150	212
Wall cabinets, 12" deep, 36" wide	4	Ea.	0.70	2.80	262	28.50	1,048	114	1,162
Wall cabinets, one door	2	Ea.	0.79	1.58	290	32	580	64	644
Over stove cabinet & microwave cabinet	1	Ea.	0.70	0.70	262	28.50	262	29	291
Over refrigerator cabinet	1	Ea.	0.67	0.67	262	27	262	27	289
Base cabinets, 24" deep, 36" wide	3	Ea.	0.79	2.37	500	32	1,500	96	1,596
Base cabinet, one door, one drawer	1	Ea.	0.72	0.72	390	29	390	29	419
Sink base cabinet	1	Ea.	0.79	0.79	390	32	390	32	422
Solid surface countertop	21	L.F.	1.07	22.47	112	43.50	2,352	914	3,266
Solid surface kitchen sink	1	Ea.	4	4	440	163	440	163	603
Valance board over sink	4	L.F.	0.04	0.16	8.90	1.65	36	7	43
Trim, cornice molding, stock pine, 9/16" x 2-1/4"	30	L.F.	0.03	0.90	0.91	1.09	27	33	60
Paint, ceiling & walls, primer	320	S.F.			0.05	0.14	16	45	61
Paint, ceiling & walls, 1 coat	320	S.F.	0.01	3.20	0.05	0.22	16	70	86
Hardwood flooring	50	S.F.	0.05	2.50	3.30	1.92	165	96	261
Sand and finish flooring	50	S.F.	0.03	1.50	0.76	0.80	38	40	78
Paint, cornice trim, simple design, incl. puttying, primer	30	L.F.	0.01	0.30	0.03	0.44	1	13	14
Paint, cornice trim, simple design, one coat	30	L.F.	0.01	0.30	0.03	0.44	1	13	14
Cooking range, freestanding, 48" wide	1	Ea.	12	12	10500	460	10,500	460	10,960
Stainless steel hood for range	1	Ea.	4	4	1050	166	1,050	166	1,216
Stainless steel refrigerator	1	Ea.	5.33	5.33	6325	157	6,325	157	6,482
Dishwasher, built-in, 2 cycle	1	Ea.	5	5	600	222	600	222	822
Pantry framing	12	L.F.	0.16	1.92	3.69	6.50	44	78	122
Pantry blocking	40	L.F.	0.03	1.20	0.37	1.30	15	52	67
Pantry gypsum wallboard	128	S.F.	0.02	2.56	0.28	0.68	36	87	123
Pantry gypsum wallboard corner bead	15	L.F.	0.02	0.30	0.13	0.82	2	12	14
Pantry door	1	Ea.	0.80	0.80	246	32.50	246	33	279
Pantry lockset	1	Ea.	0.67	0.67	45	27	45	27	72
Pantry door moldings	1	Set	0.47	0.47	32	19.20	32	19	51
Pantry baseboard moldings	22	L.F.	0.03	0.66	1.68	1.36	37	30	67
Prime pantry door and trim	100	L.F.	0.01	1	0.03	0.44	3	44	47
Paint pantry door and trim	100	L.F.	0.01	1	0.03	0.44	3	44	47
Prime pantry gypsum wallboard	100	S.F.			0.05	0.14	5	14	19
Paint pantry gypsum wallboard	100	S.F.	0.01	1	0.11	0.36	11	36	47
Pantry shelving	16	L.F.	0.08	1.28	3.31	3.10	53	50	103

Project Estimate (cont.)

Description	Quantity		Labor		Cost per Unit		Total Cost		
	Quantity	Unit	Labor Hrs Per Unit	Labor Hrs Total	Material Per Unit	Installation Per Unit	Material Total	Installation Total	Total
Subcontract									
Remove existing sink & cap pipes	1	Ea.	1.14	1.14		50.50		51	51
Kitchen faucet	1	Ea.	0.80	0.80	56.50	35.50	57	36	93
Rough-in, supply, waste & vent for sink & dishwasher	2	Ea.	7.48	14.96	115	298	230	596	826
Remove existing light fixture and deactivate circuit	1	Ea.	0.26	0.26		11.45		11	11
Recessed light fixtures	6	Ea.	0.29	1.74	59.50	12.70	357	76	433
Lighting circuits	6	Ea.	0.25	1.50	4.87	11.10	29	67	96
Undercabinet light, 24" fluorescent strip	4	Ea.	0.33	1.32	58.50	14.80	234	59	293
GFI outlets	5	Ea.	0.65	3.25	38.50	29	193	145	338
Dumpster	2	Week	1	2	365	32.50	730	65	795
Subtotals							28,494	5,514	34,008
General Requirements (Site Overhead)						12%	3,419	662	4,081
Subtotals							31,913	6,176	38,089
Overhead and Profit						10%	3,191	618	3,809
Subtotals							35,104	6,794	41,898

Grand Total $41,898

Alternates

	Unit	Total Cost
Countertop materials		
Plastic laminate	L.F.	$39
Marble	L.F.	$114
Maple butcher block	L.F.	$80
Granite	L.F.	$147
Ceramic tile	L.F.	$42
Stainless steel	S.F.	$146
Kitchen sinks		
Single bowl porcelain enamel on cast iron	Ea.	$340
Double bowl porcelain enamel on cast iron	Ea.	$450
Single bowl stainless steel	Ea.	$520
Double bowl stainless steel	Ea.	$810
Single bowl enameled steel	Ea.	$235
Double bowl enameled steel	Ea.	$294
Accessories		
Garbage disposal	Ea.	$205
Single control lever handle faucet, with pull-out spray, white	Ea.	$238
Single control lever handle faucet, with pull-out spray, polished chrome	Ea.	$219
Single control lever handle faucet, with pull-out spray, polished brass	Ea.	$256
Backsplash options		
Plastic laminate	S.F.	$6
Ceramic tile	S.F.	$8
Stainless steel	S.F.	$7
Flooring		
Floating laminate flooring	S.F.	$6
Sheet vinyl flooring	S.F.	$5
Linoleum flooring	S.F.	$6
12" x 12" ceramic tile flooring	S.F.	$6
Stone flooring	S.F.	$43

Project Worksheet

	Unit	Quantity	Price per Unit	Total	Dimensions	Source/Model#/ Specs

Project Worksheet

Part Three

Baths

Bathroom Remodeling

This part of the book contains estimates for sample bath projects, from replacing a fixture to complete renovations of half, full, and master baths. Like the Kitchens section, each estimate comes with:

- A materials list

- Typical labor-hours (contractor and subcontractors) for the tasks involved

- Total cost, including overhead and profit*

- Things to consider if you're planning a similar job

- Floor plans showing the layout of the model project that was estimated

- And, for most whole room renovations, a blank Project Worksheet that you can use to list, count, and price the items needed for your particular jobs.

Use the "Location Factors" at the back of the book to easily adjust costs to your specific location.

These estimates give you a reference point if you're talking over a possible project with a homeowner, but are not ready to bid it yet. You can also use them as a check on your own bid pricing to make sure you're in the ballpark and that you've included all major items.

Following are tips for bath design and fixtures, based on recommendations from the National Kitchen & Bath Association (NKBA) and other sources.

Look for additional information with each project estimate. Also see "Estimating the Project" at the beginning of this book for things to check during the site visit.

Planning & Design

Clearances: Suggested Guidelines

Toilets

- A minimum clearance of 15" from the center of the toilet to a wall, vanity, or tub next to it, on both sides.

- A minimum of 30" × 48" floor space in front of the fixture. Up to a foot of this space can be under an adjacent lavatory.

- A minimum of 36" × 66" for separate toilet areas/compartments.

Vanities & Lavatories

- Standard vanity heights: 30"-34".

- 15" minimum clearance from the center of the sink to a wall or fixtures.

- 30" minimum between the centers of two sinks.

- Appropriate knee space.

- Mirrors over lavatories generally no more than 40" above the floor.

- 30" × 48" clear floor space minimum parallel or at a right angle to the lavatory.

Tubs

- Standard tub length: 60"; width is 30" to 32".

- Clear floor space next to tub: If parallel to tub, at least 60" × 30". If perpendicular to tub, at least 60" × 48".

- A minimum of 15" extra clear floor space if a built-in seat is planned on one end of the tub.

- An extra 12" to 18" of clear floor space adjacent to the control panel on whirlpool tubs that have these panels.

"Opening Up" the Space

Most bath renovations involve working with the existing bathroom space, in many cases no more than 50 SF. Homeowners tend to want a more spacious look and feel for their new bathroom, along with an update of fixtures and finishes. Here are some ideas:

Vanities take up a lot of space, visually and in square feet of floor area. If vanity storage space is essential, a pedestal sink won't work, but a smaller or shallower vanity with less counter space might be an option. Another solution might be small corner vanity, though additional plumbing rough-in will be involved in a location change. If the owner must have a larger vanity, you might suggest one that is raised on legs. It will look less bulky, as more of the floor will show.

Counters, if part of the design, should flow smoothly, for example, unifying the vanity with the toilet tank and/or storage cabinet.

Mirrors and reflective surfaces, including glass shelves and glass-doored cabinets, are classic solutions.

Color scheme and uniformity of materials play a role in giving the room a "clean" look that maximizes the space visually. Staying with simple, unified, neutral colors is a big help. Also, avoid mixing too many materials. For example, instead of a wood vanity with an enameled sink, tile countertop, printed wallpaper, painted beadboard, vinyl flooring, and a fiberglass tub surround, you might suggest that the homeowner stick with just a couple of these materials.

Windows—a new or larger window, a greenhouse window, a skylight, or even a solar "tube" (if there isn't enough space for a skylight) help open and brighten the space.

New light fixtures can increase a bathroom's spacious feeling. Bright lights, if directed at a pale wall or floor, give a feeling of more space. Up-lights can make a low ceiling appear higher. Dimmer switches are becoming popular in every room, including the bath.

Placement of fixtures is key to not only a spacious look, but un-cramped function. Ideally, the toilet should not be placed opposite the entry door, and of course you need to allow for "swing space" for the entry, shower, and vanity doors, as well as open casement windows. Keep rough-in costs in mind if you're moving fixtures.

Other Design Considerations

Bathroom floor coverings should be able to withstand regular exposure to water, safe to walk on when wet, and easy to clean. Wall coverings should be water-resistant, and paint should be washable.

Ground-fault-interrupter electrical outlets are required. For a master bath, you may need two outlets, one for each sink/vanity area.

Fixture Facts

- **Quality/Budget:** Authorities like the NKBA recommend that homeowners purchase the best quality fixtures their budgets can afford since sinks, tubs, showers, and toilets are typically expected to last for many years. The homeowner may want to consider how long they expect to remain in the home and the effect of fixture quality on resale value in making these decisions.

- **Drop-in or pedestal sinks** start at $60-$120. Solid surface vanities with sinks are about $200-$500. Large or more elaborate pedestal sinks can cost up to $1,000. Furniture-quality models can be $1,000 or more. Basic chrome, two-handle faucets are about $50-$100, while solid-brass and single-lever controls tend to fall between $100 and $300. Designer styles and other metals, like brushed nickel or pewter, can be $300 or more.

- **Tubs:** Enameled cast iron is durable, but cast acrylic and fiberglass are lighter and come in more shapes and with more features. Tubs next to a wall are usually 32" × 60", although you can also get widths from 24" to 42". Corner tubs are about 48" on the side next to the wall. Tubs can be placed at floor level, raised on a platform, or sunk into the floor. Additional framing may be needed if the estimated total weight of a cast iron bathtub, in use, exceeds 30 lbs/SF.

A standard 5' fiberglass or enameled-steel tub runs around $100-$150, and acrylic tubs $150-$400. Cast iron models can be several hundred dollars. Soaking tubs on ornamental feet, as well as extra long and deep tubs, are more expensive.

- **Whirlpool tubs** are made of the same materials as regular tubs. Rectangular models range from standard tub-size up to 48" × 84". Basic whirlpools are priced at roughly $400. Bigger tubs with more jets and a more powerful motor generally cost between $500-$1,000. Higher-end models with more bells and whistles, such as heaters, variable-speed pumps, and digital controls, run from $2,000-$5,000.

A whirlpool contains a pump to circulate the water through jets around the sides. Units that don't come with a heater draw hot water from the home's water heater. Find out the estimated total weight of the whirlpool tub when in use. If more than 30 lbs/SF, you may need to strengthen the framing to support the additional load.

- **Shower stalls,** usually 32" or 36" square, start at around $100-$200 for low-end aluminum models. Acrylic or fiberglass units, and those with angled shapes are around $300-$1,000. Kits that include glass doors, solid-surface panel walls, and a base run between $1,000-$3,000.

Plumbing

- **Faucets for tubs and showers:** A tub/shower faucet with a bath spout and a fixed shower head starts at about $75-$100. Adjustable-height shower heads with handheld sprayers and anti-scald devices cost around $200-$400. Tub faucets range from basic at $100 to Roman styles at $400 or so. Multiple shower jets range from around $100 for a dual head unit to $1,500 or more.

- **Toilets** (economy models—two-piece, gravity-fed, white—as well as some elongated models) are less than $100. One-piece units with pressure-assisted flush are $300-$700. Higher-end models with brass hardware, quiet flush, and colors can cost $800-$1,500.

- **Venting:** New bath fixtures require it—both rooftop vents to let air into the drain-waste-vent system and also a fan ventilation system in a full bath, if there's no window.

- **Access panels:** In a new or completely remodeled bathroom, plan to provide access panels to piping in the wall. If new exterior piping is to be buried, protect it, wrap it, and make sure it's accessible for future service.

- **Soldering precautions:** If soldering pipes, remove flammable materials from the area, and have a fire extinguisher handy. Watch the area around the piping for any signs of smoke or fire, especially in a confined area or where hot material could drop into a wall or floor cavity.

- **Pre-assembly of piping components,** whenever practical, makes final installations easier.

- **Supply and waste piping problems,** depending on the age of the home, may need to be corrected before you can do the rough-in for new fixtures.

Pedestal Lavatory

Remove old vanity/sink and replace with new pedestal lavatory.

Pedestal sinks, or "lavatories," are popular in half baths because they can dress up the room and make a small area look more spacious. The disadvantage is lack of counter and storage space that a vanity cabinet would provide, but this is usually not a big factor in a half bath.

Installing pedestal lavatories can be a challenge in a remodel because the waste and water pipe rough-in locations have to be close together in order for the

pipes to be hidden behind the pedestal. It may be necessary to relocate the piping within the wall to meet this requirement.

Some pedestal lavatories need backing in the wall behind them, similar to the backing needed for wall-hung sinks. The backing provides for the bracket that will partly support the lavatory.

This project estimate includes removal of an existing vanity base and subcontracted plumbing work; namely removal of the old lavatory and the

rough-in of supply, waste, and vent, and installation of the new unit. The materials include a moderately priced new pedestal lavatory and a standard center-set faucet.

Check the "Alternates" box for costs for higher-end faucets (center-set vs. single lever), including chrome, polished brass, and black nickel.

Project Estimate

Description	Quantity		Labor		Cost per Unit		Total Cost		
	Quantity	Unit	Labor Hrs Per Unit	Labor Hrs Total	Material Per Unit	Installation Per Unit	Material Total	Installation Total	Total
Self-Performed									
Remove existing vanity base	3	L.F.	0.20	0.60		5.90		18	18
Subcontract									
Remove existing lavatory	1	Ea.	1	1		44.50		45	45
Alter rough plumbing	1	Ea.	6.96	6.96	99.50	277	100	277	377
New pedestal lavatory	1	Ea.	3.90	3.90	700	156	700	156	856
Faucet	1	Set	0.80	0.80	123	35.50	123	36	159
Subtotals							923	532	1,455
General Requirements (Site Overhead)						12%	111	64	175
Subtotals							1,034	596	1,630
Overhead and Profit						10%	103	60	163
Subtotals							1,137	656	1,793

Grand Total $1,793

Alternates

	Unit	Total Cost
Lavatory faucets		
Cross handle polished chrome faucet and pop-up drain	Ea.	$174
Cross handle polished brass faucet and pop-up drain	Ea.	$235
Single lever black nickel faucet and pop-up drain	Ea.	$286
Single lever polished brass faucet and pop-up drain	Ea.	$286
Single lever polished chrome faucet and pop-up drain	Ea.	$208

Single Lavatory Placement

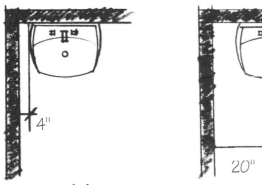

Recommended:
The distance from the centerline of the lavatory to the sidewall/tall obstacle should be at least 20".

Code Requirement:
* The minimum distance from the centerline of the lavatory to a wall is 15". (IPC 405.3.1)

* The minimum distance between a wall and the edge of a freestanding or wall-hung lavatory is 4". (IRC R 307.2)

Based on guidelines published by the National Kitchen & Bath Association

Vanity & Lavatory

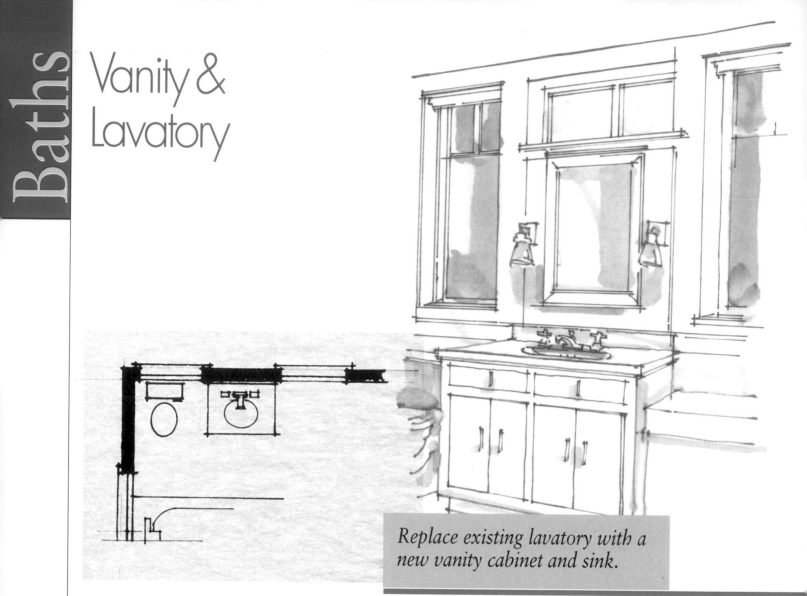

Replace existing lavatory with a new vanity cabinet and sink.

Vanities offer some advantages over pedestal lavatory installations, as the cabinet easily covers the rough-in, as well as any evidence of where the old lavatory or vanity was once connected. Installations can be complicated, though, if there is damage from dampness or rot, or if there are problems with the shut-off valves or drain pipe.

The three vanity components—cabinet, counter, and sink—mean a lot of choices for the homeowner... and this requires time for decision-making. Vanity cabinets are framed or frameless, stock, semi-custom, and custom in a choice of wood or composite materials. Stock vanity cabinets come in two basic depths—18" or 21", in widths from

18" to 72" (in 3" or 6" increments), and in heights from 28" to 36". A new trend is retrofitting a piece of furniture, such as a small, sometimes antique sideboard or chest, to accept a lavatory and faucet fittings. Manufacturers also make vanity cabinets with an antique furniture look and the advantage of protective finishes.

You'll need to establish whether the lavatory and counter will be solid surface or molded—with the lavatory integrated into the countertop, or if it will be a counter with a drop-in lavatory of china, cast iron, enameled steel or other metals, fiberglass, or stone.

If it's a drop-in lavatory, you'll need to know whether it will be self-rimming, under-mounted, or rimmed. Or it might be one of the new "vessel" sinks that sit on top of the vanity counter/cabinet.

This project estimate includes removal of an existing lavatory and installation of a hardwood vanity cabinet with a molded cultured marble top and integrated lavatory. Costs are also listed for rough-in and piping, and a chrome faucet.

The "Alternates" box includes costs for different sizes of vanity cabinets, and different counter, sink, and faucet materials.

Project Estimate

Description	Quantity		Labor		Cost per Unit		Total Cost		
	Quantity	Unit	Labor Hrs Per Unit	Labor Hrs Total	Material Per Unit	Installation Per Unit	Material Total	Installation Total	Total
Self-Performed									
Vanity base cabinet, two doors, hardwood face	1	Ea.	1	1	223	41	223	41	264
Subcontract									
Remove existing lavatory	1	Ea.	1	1		44.50		45	45
Vanity top, cultured marble, 25" x 32", single bowl	1	Ea.	2.50	2.50	196	99.50	196	100	296
Alter plumbing	1	Ea.	6.96	6.96	99.50	277	100	277	377
Center set faucet	1	Set	0.80	0.80	123	35.50	123	36	159
Subtotals							642	499	1,141
General Requirements (Site Overhead)						12%	77	60	137
Subtotals							719	559	1,278
Overhead and Profit						10%	72	56	128
Subtotals							791	615	1,406

Grand Total $1,406

Alternates

	Unit	Total Cost
Lavatory faucets		
Cross handle polished chrome faucet and pop-up drain	Ea.	$174
Cross handle polished brass faucet and pop-up drain	Ea.	$235
Single lever black nickel faucet and pop-up drain	Ea.	$286
Single lever polished brass faucet and pop-up drain	Ea.	$286
Single lever polished chrome faucet and pop-up drain	Ea.	$208
Vanity cabinets		
Vanity bases, 2 doors, 30" high, 21" deep, 24" wide, average grade	Ea.	$227
Vanity bases, 2 doors, 30" high, 21" deep, 24" wide, custom grade	Ea.	$325
Vanity bases, 2 doors, 30" high, 21" deep, 30" wide, average grade	Ea.	$264
Vanity bases, 2 doors, 30" high, 21" deep, 30" wide, custom grade	Ea.	$365
Vanity bases, 2 doors, 30" high, 21" deep, 36" wide, average grade	Ea.	$345
Vanity bases, 2 doors, 30" high, 21" deep, 36" wide, custom grade	Ea.	$525
Vanity bases, 2 doors, 30" high, 21" deep, 48" wide, average grade	Ea.	$410
Vanity bases, 2 doors, 30" high, 21" deep, 48" wide, custom grade	Ea.	$600
Vanity countertops/sinks		
Solid surface top/lavatory, 25" wide	Ea.	$251
Solid surface top/lavatory, 31" wide	Ea.	$299
Solid surface top/lavatory, 37" wide	Ea.	$340
Solid surface top/lavatory, 49" wide	Ea.	$465
Plastic laminate top	L.F.	$34
Granite top	L.F.	$147
Enameled steel lavatory	Ea.	$234
Vitreous china lavatory	Ea.	$276
Porcelain enamel on cast iron lavatory	Ea.	$340

Toilet (Water Closet)

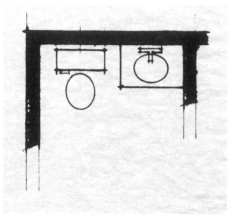

Remove and replace toilet (water closet).

eplacing a toilet starts with selecting the unit. While all toilets manufactured since 1994 are low-flow (maximum of 1.6 gallons per flush), there are some choices in toilet styles and features:

- Two-piece with a water tank above the bowl—harder to install, less expensive.

- One-piece, or "low-profile"—quieter, easier to install and clean, more expensive.

- Elongated one- and two-piece models—take up about 2" more space from front to back, mid- to high-priced.

- Pressure-assisted—use compressed air to increase the force/speed of the water, louder flush, more expensive.

- Vacuum flush—two chambers make a vacuum that pushes the water into the bowl and trap.

Toilets are also available with a higher seat (16"-18" vs. the standard 14"). These are recommended for tall users, seniors and others with limited mobility, and wheelchair users.*

In planning toilet placement, keep in mind that a minimum of 15" of clear space should be allowed from the center of the toilet to other fixtures or obstructions. There should be a space of 30" × 48" in front of the toilet, and a minimum of 1" between the toilet tank and the wall. Toilet paper holders should be 6" past the toilet seat front and 26" above the floor. Half- or full-height walls are popular as a privacy screen in new and remodeled baths.

Also, keep in mind that, for all toilets, insulation is a good idea to reduce condensation problems.

The distance from the wall to the center of the drainpipe is a crucial dimension in a toilet replacement job. (Standard is 12", but they also can be found at 10" and 14".) The new toilet's roughing-in size can be less than that of the old fixture, but if it's greater, the new toilet won't fit.

This project estimate includes a basic two-piece toilet and installation parts. It's assumed that no additional rough-in work is required. See the "Alternates" box for costs for a low-profile toilet and a bidet.

See the Accessible (Barrier-Free) Family Bath project for more on the requirements of wheelchair users.

Project Estimate

Description	Quantity		Labor		Cost per Unit		Total Cost		
	Quantity	Unit	Labor Hrs Per Unit	Labor Hrs Total	Material Per Unit	Installation Per Unit	Material Total	Installation Total	Total
Self-Performed									
Remove existing water closet	1	Ea.	1	1		44.50		45	45
Water closet, close-coupled, standard 2 piece	1	Ea.	3.02	3.02	179	120	179	120	299
Seat, plastic	1	Ea.	0.33	0.33	23	14.75	23	15	38
Closet flange and ring	1	Ea.	0.94	0.94	62.50	37.50	63	38	101
Wax ring	1	Ea.	0.08	0.08	1.09	3.69	1	4	5
Subtotals							266	222	488
General Requirements (Site Overhead)						12%	32	27	59
Subtotals							298	249	547
Overhead and Profit						10%	30	25	55
Subtotals							328	274	602

Grand Total $602

Alternates

	Unit	Total Cost
Toilet/bidet		
Low-profile toilet	Ea.	$555
Bidet	Ea.	$760

Toilet Clearances

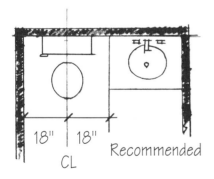

18" 18"
CL   Recommended

Recommended:
The distance from the centerline of toilet and/or bidet to any bath fixture, wall, or other obstacle should be at least 18".

Code Requirement:
A minimum distance of 15" is required from the centerline of toilet and/or bidet to any bath fixture, wall, or other obstacle. (IRC R 307.2, IRC P 2705.1.5, IPC 405.3.1)

Based on guidelines published by the National Kitchen & Bath Association

Whirlpool Tub

Remove old plumbing partition, frame new one, and install whirlpool tub and faucets.

The type of whirlpool tub that can be added as a remodel is usually limited by available space, unless the bathroom is a new addition or part of a major renovation. Space restrictions will determine tub size and shape. Sunken tubs flush with the floor clearly won't work in second-floor installations. Nevertheless, there are still several choices to be made.

Fiberglass tubs are lightweight and the least expensive, but susceptible to scratches and wear (although models with an acrylic finish have better durability). Solid acrylic tubs are more expensive, also lightweight, and more durable than fiberglass. Cast iron with an enamel coating is extremely durable,

but because of its weight, is not recommended for a large tub.

Whirlpool shapes are standard, round, square, or sculptured. The standard size is 30" or 32" × 60". Available widths are 24" to 48"; lengths are up to 84". Be sure to compare the tub's measurements against those of the hallways, doorways, and stairways along the access route to make sure the tub can get to its intended location.

Since size also determines how much water a tub uses, the capacity of the home's existing water heater is a factor. Some whirlpools come with their own heaters, but community water shortages and utility expenses should still weigh into the homeowner's selection of tub size.

Find out the tub's estimated weight when in use, so you can factor the cost of any added support framing into your estimate. Other issues to consider are how you will provide access to the motor and other parts that may need maintenance and repair in the future, and whether the existing electrical service can handle a circuit to power the motor.

This project estimate covers a molded fiberglass whirlpool tub and fittings, framing for the new tub plumbing wall, and the materials and labor needed to build a new ceramic tile shower surround.

Project Estimate

Description	Quantity		Labor		Cost per Unit		Total Cost		
	Quantity	Unit	Labor Hrs Per Unit	Labor Hrs Total	Material Per Unit	Installation Per Unit	Material Total	Installation Total	Total
Self-Performed									
Remove gypsum wallboard	30	S.F.	0.01	0.30		0.24		7	7
Remove existing plumbing partition	24	S.F.	0.01	0.24		0.39		9	9
Remove debris	3	C.Y.	0.67	2.01		19.65		59	59
Frame new plumbing partition	3	L.F.	0.16	0.48	3.69	6.50	11	20	31
Cementitious backerboard for ceramic tile walls	66	S.F.	0.05	3.30	1.15	1.86	76	123	199
Ceramic tile walls	66	S.F.	0.08	5.28	2.30	2.76	152	182	334
Curtain rod, stainless steel, 5' long, 1" diameter	1	Ea.	0.62	0.62	33.50	25	34	25	59
Subcontract									
Remove combination tub/shower	1	Ea.	1.33	1.33		59		59	59
Whirlpool tub	1	Ea.	16	16	2550	640	2,550	640	3,190
Fittings for tub & shower	1	Set	7.73	7.73	156	310	156	310	466
Dumpster	1	Week	1	1	251	32.50	251	33	284
Subtotals							3,230	1,467	4,697
General Requirements (Site Overhead)						12%	388	176	564
Subtotals							3,618	1,643	5,261
Overhead and Profit						10%	362	164	526
Subtotals							3,980	1,807	5,787

Grand Total $5,787

Shower

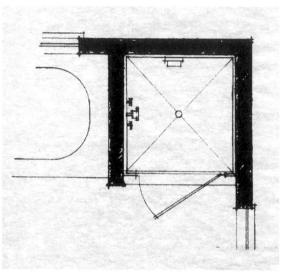

Remove old tub/shower unit and partition. Frame and install new shower.

There are an amazing number and variety of features in today's showers, from multiple, programmable shower heads, to massaging sprays, to steam—not to mention the materials used for the shower surround and doors. Prefabricated shower stalls are acrylic, fiberglass, or solid surface. Custom treatments include ceramic tile, solid surface, glass block, and any of several different types of stone. Doors range from a $100 plexiglass unit with an aluminum frame to thousands of dollars for hand-etched safety glass.

A shower space at least 36" × 36" is recommended for safety and comfort, although 32" × 32" units are often installed to accommodate space restrictions. Shelves in the unit should be recessed since anything that protrudes can be dangerous in the event of a fall.

If you're installing a fiberglass or acrylic molded shower unit, compare its measurements against doorway, hall, and stairway clearances to make sure there won't be an access problem.

The shower control should be positioned so that it's easily reached from outside the unit, not necessarily centered under the shower head.

Shower heads range from a simple $5 water-saving unit, to high-end, programmable models. Hand-held attachments are great for children's baths or disabled residents.

Shower bars with multiple nozzles may not be practical depending on the home's water pressure, the need for larger water supply lines, high utility company rates, or seasonal water shortages. If the home's water is from a well or cistern, there may be restrictions about high-volume water use fixtures, such as large whirlpool baths or multiple-head showers.

Removing the old tub can be a major operation, particularly if it's cast iron. Some tubs, if they have no salvage value, can be broken up with a sledgehammer, which can make removal easier. If you do this, don't forget precautions including wearing eye and skin protection, removing breakables from the home's walls, and being careful not to damage the ceiling or surrounding walls.

This project estimate starts with removal of the old tub/shower unit and controls, as well as gypsum wallboard and the old plumbing partition. The new installation includes a shower pan and new controls with a new mixing valve and the materials needed for the ceramic tile surround. The "Alternates" box provides costs for prefabricated fiberglass and solid surface shower stalls, and for a shower bar with multiple nozzles.

Project Estimate

Description	Quantity		Labor		Cost per Unit		Total Cost		
	Quantity	Unit	Labor Hrs Per Unit	Labor Hrs Total	Material Per Unit	Installation Per Unit	Material Total	Installation Total	Total
Self-Performed									
Remove gypsum wallboard	33	S.F.	0.01	0.33		0.24		8	8
Remove existing plumbing partition	24	S.F.	0.01	0.24		0.39		9	9
Remove debris	1	C.Y.	0.67	0.67		19.65		20	20
Frame new plumbing partition	3	L.F.	0.16	0.48	3.69	6.50	11	20	31
Gypsum wallboard	24	S.F.	0.02	0.48	0.28	0.68	7	16	23
Cementitious backerboard for ceramic tile walls	72	S.F.	0.05	3.60	1.15	1.86	83	134	217
Ceramic tile walls	72	S.F.	0.08	5.76	2.30	2.76	166	199	365
Tempered glass shower door	1	Ea.	8	8	770	355	770	355	1,125
Subcontract									
Remove combination tub/shower	1	Ea.	1.33	1.33		59		59	59
Shower pan with drain	1	Ea.	8.89	8.89	960	355	960	355	1,315
Shower pan back-up flashing	36	S.F.	0.05	1.80	1.19	1.93	43	69	112
Fittings for shower	1	Set	7.73	7.73	156	310	156	310	466
Shower mixing valve	1	Ea.	1	1	266	44.50	266	45	311
Dumpster	1	Week	1	1	251	32.50	251	33	284
Subtotals							2,713	1,632	4,345
General Requirements (Site Overhead)						12%	326	196	521
Subtotals							3,039	1,828	4,866
Overhead and Profit						10%	304	183	487
Subtotals							3,343	2,011	5,353

Grand Total $5,353

Alternates

	Unit	Total Cost
Shower enclosures		
36" Square fiberglass shower stall	Ea.	$770
32" Square polypropylene	Ea.	$780
60" Long fiberglass unit with corner seat	Ea.	$1,050
Shower accessories		
Multiple shower head column/bar	Ea.	$1,150

Lighting Upgrade

Install *new fixtures*, *switches*, and GFI outlets.

The trend for new and remodeled bathrooms is brighter, larger spaces, with a combination of well-thought-out light fixtures. Among the possibilities are a central chandelier, recessed lights, a light bar over the sink, wall sconces, and indirect light fixtures that bounce light off the ceiling or walls. Bathroom task lights include vanity/lavatory mirror lighting and fixtures over the tub and shower.

Once the basic layout of the remodeled bathroom is established, the homeowner should begin the fixture selection process. Lead times should be taken into account for specialty fixtures.

It's important to consider how the lighting will be affected by the room's finish colors. For example, an overhead-only fixture at the sink might work well with light-colored walls, sink, and counter, as the light bounces to prevent shadows. Dark walls require more—and more directional—lighting.

If fluorescent tubes are used, they should be of a type designed for vanity illumination or daylight-spectrum light, to avoid a "cold," harsh effect. (Keep in mind that fluorescent lights don't usually work with dimmer switches.)

For lights on either side of the mirror, two 60 or 75 watt bulbs are recommended. A ceiling fixture should ideally provide 100-120 watts of light.

Codes usually require vapor-proof down-lights in an enclosed shower and bath, with their switches positioned a minimum of 6' from the tub or shower. If the toilet is in a separate compartment, a ceiling fixture with a 60 or 75 watt incandescent (or 30 or 40 watt fluorescent) bulb is recommended.

This project estimate includes material costs for a recessed light fixture, two sconces, two dimmer switches, a GFI receptacle, and junction boxes and box covers, as well as wiring. The labor includes cutting and patching gypsum wallboard and fishing the wiring to the fixtures, as well as fixture installation. The "Alternates" box provides costs for an infrared heat lamp.

Project Estimate

Description	Quantity	Unit	Labor Hrs Per Unit	Labor Hrs Total	Material Per Unit	Installation Per Unit	Material Total	Installation Total	Total
Self-Performed									
Cut out gypsum wallboard for wire installation	8	Ea.	0.33	2.64		9.80		78	78
Patch gypsum wallboard	8	Ea.	0.73	5.84	0.07	29.50	1	236	237
Subcontract									
Fish wire to new lighting	3	Ea.	0.25	0.75	4.87	11.10	15	33	48
Fish wire to new GFI outlet	1	Ea.	0.25	0.25	4.87	11.10	5	11	16
Recessed lighting	1	Ea.	1	1	93.50	44.50	94	45	139
Sconces	2	Ea.	0.20	0.40	53	8.90	106	18	124
Dimmer switches	2	Ea.	0.20	0.40	5.30	8.90	11	18	29
Plastic junction boxes	6	Ea.	0.35	2.10	3.78	15.45	23	93	116
GFI receptacle	1	Ea.	0.30	0.30	32.50	13.15	33	13	46
Box covers	3	Ea.	0.10	0.30	0.34	4.45	1	13	14
Subtotals							289	558	847
General Requirements (Site Overhead)						12%	35	67	102
Subtotals							324	625	949
Overhead and Profit						10%	32	63	95
Subtotals							356	688	1,044

Grand Total   **$1,044**

Alternates

	Unit	Total Cost
Lighting/heating		
Infrared heat lamp	Ea.	$74

NKBA Electrical & Lighting Guidelines

Electrical
All GFCI receptacles should be located at electrical appliance points of use.

Code Requirement:
- At least one GFCI protected receptacle must be installed within 36" of the outside edge of the lavatory. (IRC E 3801.6)

- All receptacles must be protected by ground-fault-circuit-interrupters (GFCI). (IRC 3802.1)

- A receptacle shall not be installed within a shower or bathtub space. (IRC E 3902.10)

- Switches shall not be installed within wet locations in tub or shower spaces unless installed as part of the listed tub or shower assembly. (IRC E 3901.7)

Lighting
In addition to general lighting, task lighting should be provided for each functional area in the bathroom (i.e. grooming, showering).

Code Requirement:
- At least one wall-switch controlled light must be provided. Switch must be placed at the entrance. (IRC E 3901.6, IRC E 3803.2)

- All light fixtures installed within tub and shower spaces should be marked "suitable for damp/wet locations." (IRC E 3903.8)

- Hanging fixtures cannot be located within a zone of 3' feet horizontally and 8' vertically from the top of the bathtub rim. (IRC E 3903.10)

Based on guidelines published by the National Kitchen & Bath Association

Ventilation

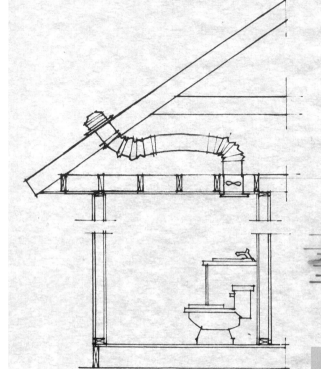

Install fan, duct, and vent.
Cut and patch ceiling and roof.

Most building codes require a window or exhaust fan in bathrooms. It's better to have both, though, in order to prevent mold, mildew, and odors, not to mention peeling paint and wallpaper, and damage to (and behind) walls. Fan styles include ceiling (with or without a light and/or infrared heater), wall, and attic-mounted. Building codes may require that the fan be placed in a certain location.

Fans should be vented to the outdoors, rather than the attic, and should go through an exterior wall or a cap on the roof. Ductwork should be insulated to prevent excessive condensation.

Fan motors are axial (propeller) or centrifugal (squirrel-cage). The fan must be the right capacity for the room size, which is determined by multiplying the room's length and width by a factor of 1.1, assuming an 8' ceiling. For a 7' × 8' bathroom, this would be:

$$7 \times 8 \times 1.1 = 61.6 \text{ cfm,}$$
or a minimum of 62 cfm.

If the exhaust ducts have to be long or contain several elbows, the fan capacity will need to be greater to overcome the added resistance.

Fans also have a noise rating, using a unit of sound called a *sone*. Fan ratings range from one sone (equal to a quiet refrigerator) to over four sones. The quieter models generally cost more. Most fans have one speed. Some high-end models have multiple speeds, as well as features such as humidity or motion sensors.

This project estimate covers the cost to install an attic-mounted, 6" diameter axial fan with an air flow rating of 110 cfm, which is a "low-noise" model. In the bathroom, sound is reduced by distance and insulation. Other materials include ductwork and a wall switch.

The "Alternates" box includes costs for supplemental heat, including a heat lamp, wall heater, and toe-kick heater for a vanity cabinet.

Project Estimate

Description	Quantity		Labor		Cost per Unit		Total Cost		
	Quantity	Unit	Labor Hrs Per Unit	Labor Hrs Total	Material Per Unit	Installation Per Unit	Material Total	Installation Total	Total
Self-Performed									
Miscellaneous interior demolition	1	Job	2	2		59		59	59
Miscellaneous exterior demolition	1	Job	2	2		59		59	59
Roof patching	1	Job	4	4		150		150	150
Flexible duct	10	L.F.	0.04	0.40	1.13	1.78	11	18	29
Roof mounted vent	1	Ea.	0.27	0.27	30.50	10	31	10	41
Subcontract									
Switch, box and cover	1	Ea.	0.47	0.47	8.90	21	9	21	30
Bathroom ventilation fan	1	Ea.	0.53	0.53	84.50	23.50	85	24	109
Vent fan wiring	1	Ea.	0.25	0.25	4.87	11.10	5	11	16
Subtotals							141	352	493
General Requirements (Site Overhead)						12%	17	42	59
Subtotals							158	394	552
Overhead and Profit						10%	16	39	55
Subtotals							174	433	607

Grand Total $607

Alternates

	Unit	Total Cost
Heating		
Heat lamp	Ea.	$191
Wall heater	Ea.	$239
Toe-kick heater	Ea.	$45

Linen Closet

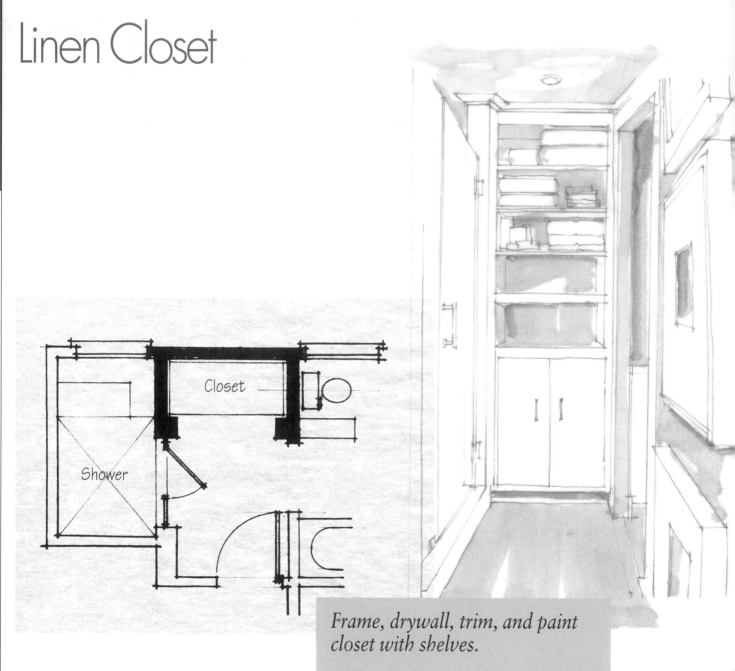

Shower

Closet

Frame, drywall, trim, and paint closet with shelves.

If the bathroom has adequate space, a linen or storage closet is an amenity almost any homeowner will greatly appreciate. Especially in a family or master bath, there can be a lot to store—from towels to cosmetics, grooming appliances, bath toys, a hamper, cleaning supplies, and even books and magazines.

If the room doesn't have space for a closet, you may be able to gain space from an adjoining room or hallway. The

installation is pretty straightforward unless there is piping or wiring in a wall that needs to be cut through to access adjoining space.

This project estimate covers the cost to construct a 2-1/2' deep by 4' wide built-in cupboard/linen closet with shelves and cabinet doors. You might want to discuss with the homeowner the possibility of adding extra features, such as drawers in the bottom of the closet, or a pull-out hamper or shelves.

The "Alternates" box provides costs for a stock cabinet, a ceiling light fixture inside the closet, and additional storage in the form of a medicine cabinet. Also included is the per SF cost for a large wall mirror to maximize the feel of the remaining space.

See also the Vanity & Lavatory project for additional storage ideas.

Project Estimate

Description	Quantity		Labor		Cost per Unit		Total Cost		
	Quantity	Unit	Labor Hrs Per Unit	Labor Hrs Total	Material Per Unit	Installation Per Unit	Material Total	Installation Total	Total
Self-Performed									
Wood framing partitions, 2 x 4	12	L.F.	0.16	1.92	3.69	6.50	44	78	122
Blocking, misc. to wood construction	40	L.F.	0.03	1.20	0.37	1.30	15	52	67
Gypsum wallboard	128	S.F.	0.02	2.56	0.28	0.68	36	87	123
Corner bead, galvanized steel, 1" x 1"	15	L.F.	0.02	0.30	0.13	0.82	2	12	14
Trim for baseboard	22	L.F.	0.03	0.66	1.68	1.36	37	30	67
Shelving, 1 x 12	16	L.F.	0.08	1.28	3.31	3.10	53	50	103
Cabinet doors	2	Ea.	0.57	1.14	49.50	23.50	99	47	146
Paint, walls and ceiling, primer	100	S.F.			0.05	0.14	5	14	19
Paint, walls and ceiling, 2 coats	100	S.F.	0.01	1	0.11	0.36	11	36	47
Paint, trim and baseboard, primer	100	S.F.	0.01	1	0.03	0.44	3	44	47
Paint, trim and baseboard, 1 coat incl. puttying	100	S.F.	0.01	1	0.03	0.44	3	44	47
Subtotals							308	494	802
General Requirements (Site Overhead)						12%	37	59	96
Subtotals							345	553	898
Overhead and Profit						10%	35	55	90
Subtotals							380	608	988

Grand Total   **$988**

Alternates

	Unit	Total Cost
Cabinetry		
48" wide stock wall cabinet	Ea.	$365
Medicine cabinet	Ea.	$100
Lighting		
Ceiling light fixture	Ea.	$133
Wiring for above	Ea.	$16
Specialties		
Mirror	S.F.	$12

Half Bath

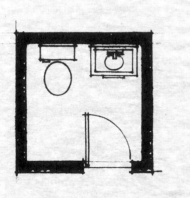

Replace fixtures and install new floor and wall tile.

Remodeling this room—whether it's called a half bath, guest bath, or powder room—has a scheduling advantage in that it's not a primary, heavily depended on facility like a family bath. Being small and having only two fixtures also limits the number of choices a homeowner has to make. And the room's small scale can provide an opportunity to splurge a little on finish materials. A disadvantage for the contractor is a cramped work space.

Although most half baths are at least 3' × 5', some are squeezed into very tight spaces under the stairs, in a former closet, and other creative locations. If

necessary and the homeowner is agreeable, scaled-down lavatories and toilets can help meet space restrictions and allow for code-required clearances. To keep smaller half baths from feeling too confined, use a pocket door or one that swings out fully. Wheelchair-accessible powder rooms need adequate space for the wheelchair's turning radius—5' diameter in the center of the room.*

If you're building a completely new half bath, try to locate it off a hallway, not directly accessed from the living, dining, or family rooms. If you have the space in a new or major remodeling project,

you can also add insulation or staggered framing to reduce sound transmission.

This project estimate starts with complete gutting of an existing 4' × 6' bathroom—removing the old walls, ceiling, insulation, and vinyl flooring, as well as the plumbing and light fixtures. All of these items are replaced with new materials and fixtures, including a pedestal lavatory and toilet, and ceramic tile flooring and walls. The "Alternates" box provides costs for stone, tile, vinyl, linoleum, and laminate flooring.

See the Accessible (Barrier-Free) Family Bath project for more on clearances.

Project Estimate

Description	Quantity		Labor		Cost per Unit		Total Cost		
	Quantity	Unit	Labor Hrs Per Unit	Labor Hrs Total	Material Per Unit	Installation Per Unit	Material Total	Installation Total	Total
Self-Performed									
Remove existing medicine cabinet	2	L.F.	0.20	0.40		5.90		12	12
Remove existing vanity cabinet	3	L.F.	0.20	0.60		5.90		18	18
Remove gypsum wallboard ceiling	24	S.F.	0.02	0.48		0.59		14	14
Remove gypsum wallboard	160	S.F.	0.01	1.60		0.24		38	38
Remove vinyl flooring	24	S.F.	0.01	0.24		0.34		8	8
Remove existing underlayment	24	S.F.	0.01	0.24		0.31		7	7
Remove insulation	11	C.F.	0.01	0.11		0.17		2	2
Remove debris to dumpster	5	C.Y.	0.67	3.35		19.65		98	98
Exterior wall insulation	32	S.F.	0.01	0.32	0.30	0.20	10	6	16
Gypsum wallboard ceiling	24	S.F.	0.02	0.48	0.28	0.85	7	20	27
Gypsum wallboard	80	S.F.	0.02	1.60	0.28	0.68	22	54	76
Cementitious backerboard walls	80	S.F.	0.05	4	1.15	1.86	92	149	241
Ceramic tile cove base	20	L.F.	0.13	2.60	3.45	4.09	69	82	151
Ceramic tile walls	80	S.F.	0.08	6.40	2.30	2.76	184	221	405
Ceramic tissue dispenser and towel bar	2	Ea.	0.20	0.40	10.65	6.40	21	13	34
Cementitious backerboard floor	24	S.F.	0.03	0.72	1.15	1.24	28	30	58
Ceramic tile flooring	24	S.F.	0.06	1.44	3.45	2.09	83	50	133
Paint, ceiling, walls & door, primer, 1 coat	162	S.F.			0.05	0.14	8	23	31
Mirror, plate glass, 30" x 34"	7	S.F.	0.10	0.70	7.10	3.88	50	27	77
Subcontract									
Remove toilet	1	Ea.	1	1		44.50		45	45
Remove lavatory	1	Ea.	1	1		44.50		45	45
Water closet, 2 piece	1	Ea.	3.02	3.02	179	120	179	120	299
Fittings for water closet	1	Set	5.25	5.25	168	209	168	209	377
Pedestal bathroom lavatory with plumbing	1	Ea.	3.90	3.90	700	156	700	156	856
Lavatory faucet and pop-up drain	1	Set	1.20	1.20	57.50	53	58	53	111
Electrical, light fixture with wiring	1	Ea.	0.27	0.27	39.50	11.85	40	12	52
Electrical, light switch	1	Ea.	1.40	1.40	32	62.50	32	63	95
Electrical, GFI outlet	1	Ea.	1.70	1.70	61.50	75.50	62	76	138
Electrical light fixture with wiring	3	Ea.	0.33	0.99	58.50	14.80	176	44	220
Dumpster	1	Week	1	1	251	32.50	251	33	284
Subtotals							2,240	1,728	3,968
General Requirements (Site Overhead)						12%	269	207	476
Subtotals							2,509	1,935	4,444
Overhead and Profit						10%	251	194	444
Subtotals							2,760	2,129	4,888

Grand Total $4,888

Alternates

	Unit	Total Cost
Flooring		
Floating laminate flooring	S.F.	$6
Sheet vinyl flooring	S.F.	$5
Linoleum flooring	S.F.	$6
12" x 12" ceramic tile flooring	S.F.	$6
Stone flooring	S.F.	$43

Family Bath Facelift

Remove old resilient flooring, tile floor and walls, and add new accessories. Paint and finish.

This is a good project for a bathroom with a functional layout and whose fixtures are in good shape (and an acceptable color). The new tiled walls and flooring are not only an upgrade in appearance from the old resilient flooring and painted walls, but provide more durable surfaces. New accessories/hardware, and a coat of paint complete the job.

As an alternative to the floor tile estimated for this model project, homeowners may want to consider new resilient, laminate, or stone tile flooring. It's important that they understand up-front the maintenance/durability issues of each, along with the cost differences.

If your customer is interested in ceramic tile, but concerned about maintaining clean-looking grout, they might opt for a darker grout color, or even a faux tile pattern in vinyl flooring. Textured ceramic tiles are less slippery. Some homeowners may be interested in adding radiant floor heating beneath the tiles.

This project estimate is based on a 7' × 8' three-fixture bathroom and includes new ceramic tile flooring and partially tiled walls. Also included are new towel bars and a toilet tissue holder, and painting of the upper walls.

Check the "Alternates" box for the costs of a new door, crown molding, or medium-quality, moisture-resistant wallpaper. There are also costs for different types of flooring, including stone, tile, laminate, linoleum, and vinyl.

Project Estimate

Description	Quantity		Labor		Cost per Unit		Total Cost		
	Quantity	Unit	Labor Hrs Per Unit	Labor Hrs Total	Material Por Unit	Installation Per Unit	Material Total	Installation Total	Total
Self-Performed									
Remove towel bar	1	Ea.	0.27	0.27		7.85		8	8
Remove toilet tissue dispenser	1	Ea.	0.27	0.27		7.85		8	8
Remove resilient flooring	36	S.F.	0.02	0.72		0.47		17	17
Remove flooring underlayment	36	S.F.	0.01	0.36		0.31		11	11
Remove debris	1	C.Y.	0.67	0.67		19.65		20	20
Ceramic tile cove base	25	L.F.	0.13	3.25	3.45	4.09	86	102	188
Ceramic tile walls	100	S.F.	0.08	8	2.30	2.76	230	276	506
Cementitious backerboard for flooring	36	S.F.	0.03	1.08	1.15	1.24	41	45	86
Ceramic tile floor	36	S.F.	0.06	2.16	3.45	2.09	124	75	199
Ceramic towel bar and tissue dispenser	2	Ea.	0.20	0.40	10.65	6.40	21	13	34
Paint walls and ceiling	176	S.F.	0.01	1.76	0.16	0.44	28	77	105
Subtotals							530	652	1,182
General Requirements (Site Overhead)						12%	64	78	142
Subtotals							594	730	1,324
Overhead and Profit						10%	59	73	132
Subtotals							653	803	1,456

Grand Total $1,456

Alternates

	Unit	Total Cost
Additional features		
Pre-hung interior door	Ea.	$310
Crown molding	L.F.	$3
Wallpaper	S.F.	$2
Flooring		
Floating laminate flooring	S.F.	$6
Sheet vinyl flooring	S.F.	$5
Linoleum flooring	S.F.	$6
12" x 12" ceramic tile flooring	S.F.	$6
Stone flooring	S.F.	$43

Family Bath Renovation

Tile walls and floors, and install new fixtures, mirror, lighting, and GFI outlets.

This project is a total renovation—gutting the room down to the studs and replacing the plumbing and light fixtures, walls, ceiling, and flooring. This approach allows for a whole new design and fixture layout and gives homeowners a lot of decisions to make. If they're not getting help from a designer, you might need to steer them toward retailers, magazines, and Web sites for the information they need.

Features that could have a big cost impact, like plumbing rough-in for new fixture locations and structural support for a large tub, should be clarified early on.

Durability, safety, storage, and counter space are always big issues in family bathrooms. Slip-resistant tile flooring, a wider medicine cabinet, a wide counter with a vanity, storage over the tub or toilet, and/or a bathroom linen closet are all good features. Surface materials and plumbing fixtures should be easy to clean.

Lighting—natural and artificial—should also be a major focus. Task, ambient, and accent lighting should be blended for the best effect. Adding a quality skylight (that will not introduce moisture problems) can brighten the space and make it feel more open.

Separating fixtures is desirable in a family bath, but space limitations in a remodel don't always allow for it. Creative (and compact) solutions like vanities placed inside a recessed area of the room, or translucent glass panels as dividers, can help.

This estimate covers the cost to gut a 7' × 8' bathroom, and to replace all plumbing and light fixtures, walls, ceiling, flooring, and finishes. The "Alternates" box provides unit costs for different types of flooring, different sized vanities, various types of sinks and faucets, and a standard medicine cabinet.

Project Estimate

Description	Quantity		Labor		Cost per Unit		Total Cost		
	Quantity	Unit	Labor Hrs Per Unit	Labor Hrs Total	Material Per Unit	Installation Per Unit	Material Total	Installation Total	Total
Self-Performed									
Remove medicine cabinet	2	L.F.	0.20	0.40		5.90		12	12
Remove vanity top	3	L.F.	0.08	0.24		2.36		7	7
Remove vanity	3	L.F.	0.20	0.60		5.90		18	18
Remove towel bar and tissue dispenser	2	Ea.	0.27	0.54		7.85		16	16
Remove gypsum wallboard ceiling	56	S.F.	0.02	1.12		0.59		33	33
Remove gypsum wallboard	286	S.F.	0.01	2.86		0.24		69	69
Remove existing plumbing partition	24	S.F.	0.01	0.24		0.39		9	9
Remove insulation	20	C.F.	0.01	0.20		0.17		3	3
Remove debris	5	C.Y.	0.67	3.35		19.65		98	98
Frame new plumbing partition	3	L.F.	0.16	0.48	3.69	6.50	11	20	31
Exterior wall insulation	56	S.F.	0.01	0.56	0.30	0.20	17	11	28
Gypsum wallboard ceiling	56	S.F.	0.02	1.12	0.28	0.85	16	48	64
Gypsum wallboard	144	S.F.	0.02	2.88	0.28	0.68	40	98	138
Cementitious backerboard for ceramic tile walls	104	S.F.	0.05	5.20	1.15	1.86	120	193	313
Vanity cabinet	1	Ea.	1.40	1.40	545	57	545	57	602
Double bowl solid surface vanity top	1	Ea.	1	1	630	41	630	41	671
Ceramic tile base	26	L.F.	0.13	3.38	3.45	4.09	90	106	196
Ceramic tile walls	104	S.F.	0.08	8.32	2.30	2.76	239	287	526
Cementitious backerboard for ceramic tile floor	1	S.F.	0.03	0.03	1.15	1.24	1	1	2
Ceramic tile floors	56	S.F.	0.06	3.36	3.45	2.09	193	117	310
Painting, ceiling, walls & door, primer	310	S.F.			0.05	0.14	16	43	59
Painting, ceiling, walls & door, 1 coat	310	S.F.	0.01	3.10	0.05	0.22	16	68	84
Curtain rod, stainless steel, 5' long, 1" diameter	1	Ea.	0.62	0.62	33.50	25	34	25	59
Mirror, plate glass, 30" x 34"	7	S.F.	0.10	0.70	7.10	3.88	50	27	77
Ceramic towel bar and tissue dispenser	1	Ea.	0.20	0.20	10.65	6.40	11	6	17
Trim, baseboard, 9/16" x 3-1/2" wide, pine	12	L.F.	0.03	0.36	1.68	1.36	20	16	36
Subcontract									
Remove combination tub/shower	1	Ea.	1.33	1.33		59		59	59
Lavatory faucet	2	Ea.	0.80	1.60	41	35.50	82	71	153
Bathtub, module/shower wall surround, molded fbgls, 5' long	1	Ea.	4	4	545	159	545	159	704
Fittings for tub & shower	1	Set	7.73	7.73	156	310	156	310	466
Water closet, 2 piece	1	Ea.	3.02	3.02	179	120	179	120	299
Fittings for water closet	1	Set	5.25	5.25	168	209	168	209	377
Electrical, 2 light fixtures with wiring	2	Ea.	0.27	0.54	39.50	11.85	79	24	103
Electrical, 2 light switches	2	Ea.	1.40	2.80	32	62.50	64	125	189
Electrical, one GFI outlet	1	Ea.	1.70	1.70	61.50	75.50	62	76	138
Dumpster	1	Week	1	1	251	32.50	251	33	284
Subtotals							3,635	2,615	6,250
General Requirements (Site Overhead)						12%	436	314	750
Subtotals							4,071	2,929	7,000
Overhead and Profit						10%	407	293	700
Subtotals							4,478	3,222	7,700

Grand Total   **$7,700**

Alternates

	Unit	Total Cost
Flooring		
Floating laminate flooring	S.F.	$6
Sheet vinyl flooring	S.F.	$5
Linoleum flooring	S.F.	$6
12" x 12" ceramic tile flooring	S.F.	$6
Stone flooring	S.F.	$43
Lavatory faucets		
Cross handle polished chrome faucet and pop-up drain	Ea.	$174
Cross handle polished brass faucet and pop-up drain	Ea.	$235
Single lever black nickel faucet and pop-up drain	Ea.	$286
Single lever polished brass faucet and pop-up drain	Ea.	$286
Single lever polished chrome faucet and pop-up drain	Ea.	$208
Vanity cabinets		
Vanity bases, 2 doors, 30" high, 21" deep, 24" wide, average grade	Ea.	$227
Vanity bases, 2 doors, 30" high, 21" deep, 24" wide, custom grade	Ea.	$325
Vanity bases, 2 doors, 30" high, 21" deep, 30" wide, average grade	Ea.	$264
Vanity bases, 2 doors, 30" high, 21" deep, 30" wide, custom grade	Ea.	$365
Vanity bases, 2 doors, 30" high, 21" deep, 36" wide, average grade	Ea.	$345
Vanity bases, 2 doors, 30" high, 21" deep, 36" wide, custom grade	Ea.	$525
Vanity bases, 2 doors, 30" high, 21" deep, 48" wide, average grade	Ea.	$410
Vanity bases, 2 doors, 30" high, 21" deep, 48" wide, custom grade	Ea.	$600
Vanity countertops/sinks		
Solid surface top/lavatory, 25" wide	Ea.	$251
Solid surface top/lavatory, 31" wide	Ea.	$299
Solid surface top/lavatory, 37" wide	Ea.	$340
Solid surface top/lavatory, 49" wide	Ea.	$465
Plastic laminate top	L.F.	$34
Granite top	L.F.	$147
Enameled steel lavatory	Ea.	$234
Vitreous china lavatory	Ea.	$276
Porcelain enamel on cast iron lavatory	Ea.	$340
Specialties		
Medicine cabinet	Ea.	$100

Project Worksheet

	Unit	Quantity	Price per Unit	Total	Dimensions	Source/Model#/ Specs

"Jack & Jill" Bath

Vanity Area

Bathing Area

Vanity Area

Renovate existing bath and closet space into dual-entry, segmented bath. Add new fixtures, lighting, and tile walls and flooring.

This layout, common in newer homes, is typically shared by two children's bedrooms. It includes a central tub/shower/toilet room with privacy doors on each side, flanked by separate vanity areas, one for each bedroom. A modification of this layout provides a vanity and toilet for each bedroom, with only the tub/shower room shared. This project is easiest to carry out in a new room addition or large-scale remodel, where space might be acquired from adjoining closets or hallways.

Safety and durability should, of course, be priorities when selecting materials for any bath used by children. Surfaces should be waterproof and easy to clean. Slip-resistant flooring, such as ceramic tile with a matte finish, is a good choice.

Smaller tiles with more grout lines are even better.

Grab bars, towel bars or rings installed close to the tub, non-scald faucets, and a flexible hand-held shower attachment are all child-friendly. Avoid pointed hooks on walls or the doors and sharp edges on countertops. Door hardware should be un-lockable from inside and out. And, of course, only GFI outlets should be used.

Bath designers recommend flexibility when it comes to decorative materials for children's baths. A coat of paint or a strippable waterproof wallpaper allows for easy changes as children grow older. Vanity hardware and accessories can be easily replaced to reflect changing tastes.

The estimate for this model project includes complete gutting and removal of fixtures, framing, doors, wiring, and materials from an existing 7' × 6' standard bath and surrounding area. The installation includes new partition walls, sub-flooring, wallboard, insulation, plumbing and light fixtures, a ventilation system, and ceramic tile walls and flooring, along with new hardware and paint. Plumbing and electrical rough-in are included to account for the complete redesign of the space. The "Alternates" box lists costs for different types of flooring.

See also the Linen Closet and Lighting Upgrade projects earlier in this section.

Project Estimate

Description	Quantity		Labor		Cost per Unit		Total Cost		
	Quantity	Unit	Labor Hrs Per Unit	Labor Hrs Total	Material Per Unit	Installation Per Unit	Material Total	Installation Total	Total
Self-Performed									
Remove interior doors	5	Ea.	0.40	2		11.80		59	59
Remove existing vanity	3	L.F.	0.20	0.60		5.90		18	18
Remove existing vanity top	3	L.F.	0.08	0.24		2.36		7	7
Remove gypsum wallboard ceiling	140	S.F.	0.02	2.80		0.59		83	83
Remove gypsum wallboard	1284	S.F.	0.01	12.84		0.24		308	308
Remove existing wall framing	492	S.F.	0.01	4.92		0.39		192	192
Remove existing flooring	140	S.F.	0.01	1.40		0.34		48	48
Remove existing underlayment	140	S.F.	0.01	1.40		0.31		43	43
Remove plywood subfloor	1	S.F.	0.01	0.01		0.54		1	1
Remove exterior wall insulation	37	C.F.	0.01	0.37		0.17		6	6
Remove debris	8	C.Y.	0.67	5.36		19.65		157	157
Plywood subfloor	140	SF Flr.	0.01	1.40	0.86	0.48	120	67	187
New interior partitions	54	L.F.	0.16	8.64	3.69	6.50	199	351	550
Exterior wall insulation	112	S.F.	0.01	1.12	0.30	0.20	34	22	56
Gypsum wallboard ceiling	140	S.F.	0.02	2.80	0.28	0.85	39	119	158
Gypsum wallboard	644	S.F.	0.02	12.88	0.28	0.68	180	438	618
Cementitious backerboard on walls	252	S.F.	0.05	12.60	1.15	1.86	290	469	759
Cementitious backerboard on floor	140	S.F.	0.03	4.20	1.15	1.24	161	174	335
Ceramic tile base	76	L.F.	0.13	9.88	3.45	4.09	262	311	573
Ceramic tile walls	252	S.F.	0.08	20.16	2.30	2.76	580	696	1,276
Ceramic tile floor	130	S.F.	0.06	7.80	3.45	2.09	449	272	721
Cast iron bathtub, faucet, shower & pop-up	1	Ea.	4	4	725	159	725	159	884
New water closets	2	Ea.	3.02	6.04	179	120	358	240	598
New pedestal lavatories, faucets and pop-ups	2	Ea.	3.90	7.80	700	156	1,400	312	1,712
Ceramic towel bars and tissue dispensers	8	Ea.	0.20	1.60	10.65	6.40	85	51	136
Bathroom medicine cabinet/mirror	2	Ea.	0.57	1.14	76.50	23.50	153	47	200
Robe hooks	2	Ea.	0.22	0.44	5.45	9.05	11	18	29
Wood base	34	L.F.	0.03	1.02	1.68	1.36	57	46	103
Pre-hung interior doors	4	Ea.	0.80	3.20	265	32.50	1,060	130	1,190
Privacy locksets	4	Ea.	0.67	2.68	55.50	27	222	108	330
Paint baseboard and door trim	170	L.F.	0.02	3.40	0.09	0.88	15	150	165
Paint walls and ceilings	784	S.F.	0.01	7.84	0.16	0.44	125	345	470
Paint doors	6	Ea.	3.20	19.20	11.75	114	71	684	755
Bi-passing closet doors, frame and trim	1	Opng.	1.60	1.60	490	65	490	65	555
Closet shelving	24	L.F.	0.11	2.64	4.54	4.66	109	112	221
Subcontract									
Remove existing water closet	1	Ea.	1	1		44.50		45	45
Remove existing lavatory	1	Ea.	1	1		44.50		45	45
Remove existing fiberglass tub/shower unit	1	Ea.	1.33	1.33		59		59	59
Rough plumbing for lavatories	2	Ea.	6.96	13.92	99.50	277	199	554	753
Rough plumbing for water closets	2	Ea.	5.25	10.50	168	209	336	418	754
Rough plumbing for bathtub	1	Ea.	7.73	7.73	156	310	156	310	466
Remove existing electrical components	5	Ea.	0.26	1.30		11.45		57	57
New lighting control switches	4	Ea.	0.55	2.20	13.20	24.50	53	98	151
New GFI outlets	3	Ea.	0.65	1.95	38.50	29	116	87	203
New bathroom exhaust fan	3	Ea.	0.67	2.01	125	29.50	375	89	464
New bathroom vanity lights	4	Ea.	0.20	0.80	53	8.90	212	36	248
New bathroom recessed light	1	Ea.	0.29	0.29	59.50	12.70	60	13	73
Rough wiring for fans and lights	8	Ea.	0.25	2	4.87	11.10	39	89	128
Dumpster	1	Week	1	1	375	32.50	375	33	408

Project Estimate (cont.)

Description	Quantity		Labor		Cost per Unit		Total Cost		
	Quantity	Unit	Labor Hrs Per Unit	Labor Hrs Total	Material Per Unit	Installation Per Unit	Material Total	Installation Total	Total
Subtotals							9,116	8,241	17,357
General Requirements (Site Overhead)						12%	1,094	989	2,083
Subtotals							10,210	9,230	19,440
Overhead and Profit						10%	1,021	923	1,944
Subtotals							11,231	10,153	21,384

Grand Total   **$21,384**

Alternates

	Unit	Total Cost
Flooring		
Floating laminate flooring	S.F.	$6
Sheet vinyl flooring	S.F.	$5
Linoleum flooring	S.F.	$6
12" x 12" ceramic tile flooring	S.F.	$6
Stone flooring	S.F.	$43

Soundproofing

Since one of the main purposes of the Jack & Jill bathroom layout is creating privacy for each of the spaces, a little extra soundproofing in the partitions can be a nice enhancement. You can do this in a couple of different ways. The simplest is to fill the wall with batts of R-11 unfaced fiberglass or rigid foam insulation. You can also install two sheets of gypsum wallboard on either side of the framing.

The most effective soundproofing is achieved with staggered framing. This requires enough space for 2x6 top and bottom plates, and staggered 2x4 studs. Studs are set at 12" OC, but staggered, so that every other stud is 24" OC on the same plane. You can weave fiberglass insulation between the studs.

Project Worksheet

	Unit	Quantity	Price per Unit	Total	Dimensions	Source/Model#/ Specs

Accessible (Barrier-Free) Family Bath

Replace plumbing fixtures and fittings, tile floor and walls, and add accessories. Install new lights and GFI outlet.

In a fully accessible bath, a person using a wheelchair must be able to use all of the fixtures and move about the room. To start with, you need an open area in the center of the room at least 5' in diameter. Doorways should be 3' wide, and the bathroom door (with a lever handle) should swing outward, not into the room. A pocket door may be needed in limited space.

There should also be 4' of clear space in front of each fixture. The toilet and sink, if they share the same wall, should ideally be 4' apart, so that there is space for a care-giver to provide assistance. Light switches should be 48" above the floor.

Countertops and lavatories should be 31"-32" high with a clear space at least 27" deep × 30" wide below. Exposed pipes beneath the sink should be

insulated. Anti-scald devices and sprayers are recommended for lavatory faucets.

Showers should have a 36" opening with no threshold, and should be a minimum of 4' × 4'. (The Americans with Disabilities Act requires roll-in showers to be 30" × 60" wide for public facilities.) Grab bars or a safety rail with blocking are usually installed in the shower, along with a built-in seat. The shower controls should be easily reachable from a seated position, from both outside and inside the shower. Two separate shower heads at two different heights can be installed, or one with a hand-held spray and a bracket.

Tubs should be configured so they facilitate transfer from a wheelchair. Specialty models have built-in seats that can be rotated and hydraulic lifts. A hand-held sprayer is another good tub feature.

An 18" high toilet is recommended, with an extension for the flush handle. The toilet paper holder should be 26" above the floor, and 7"-9" in front of the toilet. There should be grab bars with blocking in the walls next to the toilet and bathtub.

This project estimate covers the cost to remove existing bath fixtures and wall and floor coverings, and install new, accessible fixtures and fittings, along with non-slip tile flooring, and tile walls. The estimate includes specialty items such as a folding shower seat, grab bars, an anti-scald device, and a tilted mirror.

Refer to the Resources at the back of this book for more information on standards for accessible design.

Project Estimate

Description	Quantity		Labor		Cost per Unit		Total Cost		
	Quantity	Unit	Labor Hrs Per Unit	Labor Hrs Total	Material Per Unit	Installation Per Unit	Material Total	Installation Total	Total
Self-Performed									
Remove existing vanity top	6	L.F.	0.08	0.48		2.36		14	14
Remove existing vanity	6	L.F.	0.20	1.20		5.90		35	35
Remove existing gypsum wallboard ceiling	80	S.F.	0.02	1.60		0.59		47	47
Remove existing gypsum wallboard	330	S.F.	0.01	3.30		0.24		79	79
Remove existing insulation	22	C.F.	0.01	0.22		0.17		4	4
Remove existing shower partition	24	S.F.	0.01	0.24		0.39		9	9
Remove existing flooring	80	S.F.	0.01	0.80		0.34		27	27
Remove existing underlayment	80	S.F.	0.01	0.80		0.31		25	25
Remove debris	8	C.Y.	0.67	5.36		19.65		157	157
Partition for shower stall	152	L.F.	0.01	1.52	0.37	0.59	56	90	146
Blocking for grab bar support	20	L.F.	0.03	0.60	0.37	1.30	7	26	33
Gypsum wallboard ceiling	80	S.F.	0.02	1.60	0.28	0.85	22	68	90
Gypsum wallboard	132	S.F.	0.02	2.64	0.28	0.68	37	90	127
Cementitious backerboard	190	S.F.	0.05	9.50	1.15	1.86	219	353	572
Ceramic tile base	42	L.F.	0.18	7.56	3.43	5.75	144	242	386
Ceramic tile walls	190	S.F.	0.08	15.20	2.30	2.76	437	524	961
Cementitious backerboard on floor	80	S.F.	0.03	2.40	1.15	1.24	92	99	191
Ceramic tile floor	80	S.F.	0.06	4.80	3.45	2.09	276	167	443
Paint, ceiling, walls & door, primer	245	S.F.			0.05	0.14	12	34	46
Paint, ceiling, walls & door, 1 coat	245	S.F.	0.01	2.45	0.05	0.22	12	54	66
Tilting accessible mirror	1	Ea.	0.80	0.80	390	32.50	390	33	423
Towel bar, stainless steel, 30" long	2	Ea.	0.35	0.70	38.50	14.15	77	28	105
Toilet tissue dispenser, surface mounted, stainless	1	Ea.	0.27	0.27	11.90	10.85	12	11	23
Grab bars	4	Ea.	0.35	1.40	55.50	14.15	222	57	279
Folding seat	1	Ea.	0.62	0.62	31.50	25	32	25	57
Subcontract									
Remove existing lavatory	1	Ea.	1	1		44.50		45	45
Remove existing bathtub	1	Ea.	2	2		88.50		89	89
Remove existing water closet	1	Ea.	1	1		44.50		45	45
Remove existing shower unit	1	Ea.	1.33	1.33		59		59	59
Wall-hung lavatory	2	Ea.	2.29	4.58	218	91	436	182	618
Hand-held shower head and mounting hardware	2	Ea.	0.40	0.80	131	17.70	262	35	297
Shower anti-scald valve	1	Ea.	1.33	1.33	114	59	114	59	173
Shower pan	13	S.F.	0.02	0.26	0.95	0.91	12	12	24
Transition strip	2	Ea.	1.33	2.66	15.45	47.50	31	95	126
Water closet, 2 piece	1	Ea.	3.02	3.02	179	120	179	120	299
Fittings for water closet	1	Set	5.25	5.25	168	209	168	209	377
Remove existing light fixtures, switches and outlet	5	Ea.	0.26	1.30		11.45		57	57
Electrical, 2 light fixtures with wiring	2	Ea.	0.27	0.54	39.50	11.85	79	24	103
Electrical, 2 light switches	2	Ea.	1.40	2.80	32	62.50	64	125	189
Electrical, one GFI outlet	1	Ea.	1.70	1.70	61.50	75.50	62	76	138
Dumpster	1	Week	1	1	375	32.50	375	33	408
Subtotals							3,829	3,563	7,392
General Requirements (Site Overhead)						12%	459	428	887
Subtotals							4,288	3,991	8,279
Overhead and Profit						10%	429	399	828
Subtotals							4,717	4,390	9,107

Grand Total   **$9,107**

Master Bath

> *Remove old walls, ceiling, flooring, and fixtures. Install new lights, GFI outlet, and plumbing fixtures. Tile walls and floor, and paint.*

This has become one of the most popular of all home renovations because it can provide a spa-like retreat for stressed homeowners and a great return on investment when the home is re-sold. A surprising number of consumers are willing to invest in luxury features such as large glass showers, walls of programmable shower heads, elaborate windows, exercise areas, and fireplaces* for the master bath, but even modest improvements can have a major effect on the atmosphere and function of this room.

These projects can require a lot of planning, and homeowners need to sort through the options and make decisions early. Specialty materials and fixtures, from tubs and sinks to tile and lighting, can require long lead times. Your estimate will also need to account for any special construction such as additional floor support for an oversize tub, or extra heating or ventilation.

Two sinks and separate toilet, shower, and tub areas are becoming standard in new master baths. Creative tricks such as half walls that set off the toilet and also house storage cabinets, and use of glass block walls or translucent glass panels, can often solve storage, space, and privacy issues.

This project estimate covers the cost to remove plumbing and light fixtures, fittings, flooring, underlayment, walls and ceiling, and an old shower partition from a 8' × 10' bathroom. The new installation includes new drywall and ceiling; new flooring and underlayment; a pedestal sink, tub, and toilet; and light fixtures, along with an added GFI outlet.

The "Alternates" box lists costs for different types of flooring, different sizes of vanities, and various sinks, counters, and faucets.

See the "Bed & Breakfast" Gas Fireplace project in the Kitchens section of this book.

Project Estimate

Description	Quantity	Unit	Labor Hrs Per Unit	Labor Hrs Total	Material Per Unit	Installation Per Unit	Material Total	Installation Total	Total
Self-Performed									
Remove existing vanity top	6	L.F.	0.08	0.48		2.36		14	14
Remove existing vanity	6	L.F.	0.20	1.20		5.90		35	35
Remove existing gypsum wallboard ceiling	80	S.F.	0.02	1.60		0.59		47	47
Remove existing gypsum wallboard	330	S.F.	0.01	3.30		0.24		79	79
Remove existing insulation	22	C.F.	0.01	0.22		0.17		4	4
Remove existing shower partition	24	S.F.	0.01	0.24		0.39		9	9
Remove existing flooring	80	S.F.	0.01	0.80		0.34		27	27
Remove existing underlayment	80	S.F.	0.01	0.80		0.31		25	25
Remove debris	8	C.Y.	0.67	5.36		19.65		157	157
Partition for shower stall	152	L.F.	0.01	1.52	0.37	0.59	56	90	146
Gypsum wallboard ceiling	80	S.F.	0.02	1.60	0.28	0.85	22	68	90
Gypsum wallboard	132	S.F.	0.02	2.64	0.28	0.68	37	90	127
Cementitious backerboard	172	S.F.	0.05	8.60	1.15	1.86	198	320	518
Ceramic tile base	42	L.F.	0.18	7.56	3.43	5.75	144	242	386
Ceramic tile walls	172	S.F.	0.08	13.76	2.30	2.76	396	475	871
Cementitious backerboard on floor	80	S.F.	0.03	2.40	1.15	1.24	92	99	191
Ceramic tile floor	80	S.F.	0.06	4.80	3.45	2.09	276	167	443
Paint, ceiling, walls & door, primer	330	S.F.			0.05	0.14	17	46	63
Paint, ceiling, walls & door, 1 coat	330	S.F.	0.01	3.30	0.05	0.22	17	73	90
Mirror, plate glass, 30" x 34"	7	S.F.	0.10	0.70	7.10	3.88	50	27	77
Towel bar, stainless steel, 30" long	2	Ea.	0.35	0.70	38.50	14.15	77	28	105
Toilet tissue dispenser, surface mounted, stainless	1	Ea.	0.27	0.27	11.90	10.85	12	11	23
Subcontract									
Remove existing lavatories	2	Ea.	1	2		44.50		89	89
Remove existing bathtub	1	Ea.	2	2		88.50		89	89
Remove existing water closet	1	Ea.	1	1		44.50		45	45
Remove existing shower unit	1	Ea.	1.33	1.33		59		59	59
Pedestal lavatory with supply, waste, & vent	1	Ea.	3.90	3.90	700	156	700	156	856
Bathtub	1	Ea.	3.64	3.64	460	145	460	145	605
Fittings for tub and shower	2	Set	7.73	15.46	156	310	312	620	932
Water closet, 2 piece	1	Ea.	3.02	3.02	179	120	179	120	299
Fittings for water closet	1	Set	5.25	5.25	168	209	168	209	377
Remove existing light fixtures, switches, and outlet	5	Ea.	0.26	1.30		11.45		57	57
Electrical, 2 light fixtures with wiring	2	Ea.	0.27	0.54	39.50	11.85	79	24	103
Electrical, 2 light switches	2	Ea.	1.40	2.80	32	62.50	64	125	189
Electrical, one GFI outlet	1	Ea.	1.70	1.70	61.50	75.50	62	76	138
Dumpster	1	Week	1	1	375	32.50	375	33	408
Subtotals							3,793	3,980	7,773
General Requirements (Site Overhead)						12%	455	478	933
Subtotals							4,248	4,458	8,706
Overhead and Profit						10%	425	446	871
Subtotals							4,673	4,904	9,577

Grand Total $9,577

Alternates

	Unit	Total Cost
Flooring		
Floating laminate flooring	S.F.	$6
Sheet vinyl flooring	S.F.	$5
Linoleum flooring	S.F.	$6
12" x 12" ceramic tile flooring	S.F.	$6
Stone flooring	S.F.	$43
Lavatory faucets		
Cross handle polished chrome faucet and pop-up drain	Ea.	$174
Cross handle polished brass faucet and pop-up drain	Ea.	$235
Single lever black nickel faucet and pop-up drain	Ea.	$286
Single lever polished brass faucet and pop-up drain	Ea.	$286
Single lever polished chrome faucet and pop-up drain	Ea.	$208
Vanity cabinets		
Vanity bases, 2 doors, 30" high, 21" deep, 24" wide, average grade	Ea.	$227
Vanity bases, 2 doors, 30" high, 21" deep, 24" wide, custom grade	Ea.	$325
Vanity bases, 2 doors, 30" high, 21" deep, 30" wide, average grade	Ea.	$264
Vanity bases, 2 doors, 30" high, 21" deep, 30" wide, custom grade	Ea.	$365
Vanity bases, 2 doors, 30" high, 21" deep, 36" wide, average grade	Ea.	$345
Vanity bases, 2 doors, 30" high, 21" deep, 36" wide, custom grade	Ea.	$525
Vanity bases, 2 doors, 30" high, 21" deep, 48" wide, average grade	Ea.	$410
Vanity bases, 2 doors, 30" high, 21" deep, 48" wide, custom grade	Ea.	$600
Vanity countertops/sinks		
Solid surface top/lavatory, 25" wide	Ea.	$251
Solid surface top/lavatory, 31" wide	Ea.	$299
Solid surface top/lavatory, 37" wide	Ea.	$340
Solid surface top/lavatory, 49" wide	Ea.	$465
Plastic laminate top	L.F.	$34
Granite top	L.F.	$147
Enameled steel lavatory	Ea.	$234
Vitreous china lavatory	Ea.	$276
Porcelain enamel on cast iron lavatory	Ea.	$340
Plumbing		
Multiple shower head column/bar	Ea.	$1,150
Whirlpool tub	Ea.	$4,250

Project Worksheet

	Unit	Quantity	Price per Unit	Total	Dimensions	Source/Model#/ Specs

Master Bath Suite

Bath Area

Dressing Area

Grooming Area

Frame and install hardwood flooring, shelves, and rods in closet. Tile bathroom walls and floor, and install new plumbing and light fixtures, mirrors, and GFI outlets.

A remodeling project with these space requirements is usually associated with an addition or major renovation that takes over an adjoining room, hallway, and/or closets. Very high-end master bath suites might also include a "spa" area with a sauna or exercise equipment, or even a small fireplace.*

A suite of this type often incorporates more expensive materials, such as marble or limestone tiles; designer lavatories, tubs, and faucets; and furniture-quality vanity bases and mirrors. Homeowners can easily spend months researching products, gathering special items, and working with a designer to prepare for this type of project.

Each of the many elements in this space has its own special considerations. Refer to the Shower, Ventilation, Lighting Upgrade, Whirlpool Tub, and Vanity & Lavatory projects for more on material, installation, and cost considerations for each of these elements.

This project estimate includes demolition of an existing bathroom, preparation, and installation of all the fixtures, new walls and ceilings, and flooring (hardwood for a 10' × 10' closet/vanity area, ceramic tile for the bath). New light fixtures and GFI outlets are also included.

See also the "Bed & Breakfast" Gas Fireplace project in the Kitchens section.

Project Estimate

Description	Quantity	Unit	Labor Hrs Per Unit	Labor Hrs Total	Material Per Unit	Installation Per Unit	Material Total	Installation Total	Total
Self-Performed									
Remove existing vanity top	6	L.F.	0.08	0.48		2.36		14	14
Remove existing vanity	6	L.F.	0.20	1.20		5.90		35	35
Remove existing gypsum wallboard ceiling	80	S.F.	0.02	1.60		0.59		47	47
Remove existing gypsum wallboard	330	S.F.	0.01	3.30		0.24		79	79
Remove existing insulation	22	C.F.	0.01	0.22		0.17		4	4
Remove existing shower partition	24	S.F.	0.01	0.24		0.39		9	9
Remove existing flooring	80	S.F.	0.01	0.80		0.34		27	27
Remove existing underlayment	240	S.F.	0.01	2.40		0.31		74	74
Carpet removal	160	S.F.				0.05		8	8
Remove debris	9	C.Y.	0.67	6.03		19.65		177	177
Partition for shower stall	152	L.F.	0.01	1.52	0.37	0.59	56	90	146
New wall framing for closet & dressing area	36	L.F.	0.16	5.76	3.69	6.50	133	234	367
Gypsum wallboard ceiling	80	S.F.	0.02	1.60	0.28	0.85	22	68	90
Gypsum wallboard	916	S.F.	0.02	18.32	0.28	0.68	256	623	879
Cementitious backerboard	172	S.F.	0.05	8.60	1.15	1.86	198	320	518
Ceramic tile base	42	L.F.	0.18	7.56	3.43	5.75	144	242	386
Ceramic tile walls	172	S.F.	0.08	13.76	2.30	2.76	396	475	871
Cementitious backerboard on floor	80	S.F.	0.03	2.40	1.15	1.24	92	99	191
Ceramic tile floor	80	S.F.	0.06	4.80	3.45	2.09	276	167	443
Hardwood flooring	160	S.F.	0.05	8	3.30	1.92	528	307	835
Sand & finish floor	1	S.F.	0.03	0.03	0.76	0.80	1	1	2
Vanity cabinet	1	Ea.	1.40	1.40	545	57	545	57	602
Trim for door and cased openings	102	L.F.	0.03	3.06	0.94	1.36	96	139	235
Granite vanity top	1	L.F.	0.61	0.61	121	25.50	121	26	147
Jamb for cased openings	40	L.F.	0.04	1.60	6.05	1.74	242	70	312
Dressing room door	1	Ea.	0.89	0.89	156	36	156	36	192
Closet shelf and pole	2	Ea.	0.53	1.06	23	21.50	46	43	89
Paint, ceiling, walls & door, primer	1274	S.F.			0.05	0.14	64	178	242
Paint, ceiling, walls & door, 1 coat	1274	S.F.	0.01	12.74	0.05	0.22	64	280	344
Mirrors	64	S.F.	0.10	6.40	7.10	3.88	454	248	702
Towel bar, stainless steel, 30" long	4	Ea.	0.35	1.40	38.50	14.15	154	57	211
Toilet tissue dispenser, surface mounted, stainless	1	Ea.	0.27	0.27	11.90	10.85	12	11	23
Make-up vanity	6	L.F.	0.80	4.80	65	32.50	390	195	585
Subcontract									
Remove existing lavatories	2	Ea.	1	2		44.50		89	89
Remove existing bathtub	1	Ea.	2	2		88.50		89	89
Remove existing water closet	1	Ea.	1	1		44.50		45	45
Remove existing shower unit	1	Ea.	1.33	1.33		59		59	59
Vanity lavatories and faucets	2	Ea.	2.50	5	560	99.50	1,120	199	1,319
Bathtub	1	Ea.	3.64	3.64	460	145	460	145	605
Fittings for tub and shower	2	Set	7.73	15.46	156	310	312	620	932
Water closet, 2 piece	1	Ea.	3.02	3.02	179	120	179	120	299
Fittings for water closet	1	Set	5.25	5.25	168	209	168	209	377

Project Estimate (cont.)

Description	Quantity		Labor		Cost per Unit		Total Cost		
	Quantity	Unit	Labor Hrs Per Unit	Labor Hrs Total	Material Per Unit	Installation Per Unit	Material Total	Installation Total	Total
Subcontract (cont.)									
Remove existing light fixtures, switches, and outlet	5	Ea.	0.26	1.30		11.45		57	57
Electrical, 2 light fixtures with wiring	6	Ea.	0.27	1.62	39.50	11.85	237	71	308
Electrical, 2 light switches	2	Ea.	1.40	2.80	32	62.50	64	125	189
Electrical, one GFI outlet	3	Ea.	1.70	5.10	61.50	75.50	185	227	412
Dumpster	1	Week	1	1	375	32.50	375	33	408
Subtotals							7,546	6,528	14,074
General Requirements (Site Overhead)						12%	906	783	1,689
Subtotals							8,452	7,311	15,763
Overhead and Profit						10%	845	731	1,576
Subtotals							9,297	8,042	17,339

Grand Total $17,339

Project Worksheet

	Unit	Quantity	Price per Unit	Total	Dimensions	Source/Model#/Specs

Pool House Bath

Replace fixtures and add sauna. Upgrade lighting and install GFI outlets. Tile walls and floor.

Today's pool house facilities focus on fitness, relaxation, and pleasure—with a swim in the pool, a hot shower, and drinks on the patio. Pool house baths range from basic facilities like the one estimated in this project to elaborate spas with features like saunas or steam compartments, exercise equipment, and adjoining outdoor hot tubs. While some homeowners will insist on these extras, they're not likely to bring the best return on investment.

If you are planning a new pool house bath instead of replacing an old one, you may need to provide a separate hot water heater. In winter, the water heater can be turned off. In climates with below-freezing temperatures, the pool house must also be properly winterized to prevent pipes from bursting. If you're planning a sauna or steam unit, they require drainage and 220-volt electrical current.

The estimate given here is an update and upgrade of an existing pool house bath, with a new pedestal lavatory, ceramic tile floors and walls, and a prefabricated tub/shower unit. If there is space available, a tiled exercise room could be added. A wet bar and an outdoor shower are other pool house features to consider. If there is no pool house, an adjacent garage or storage room might be a candidate for conversion.

If you're designing and installing a spa facility with a hot tub, you might want to order copies of the U.S. Consumer Product Safety Commission's free safety publications for these facilities. See the Resources for more information.

Project Estimate

Description	Quantity	Unit	Labor Hrs Per Unit	Labor Hrs Total	Material Per Unit	Installation Per Unit	Material Total	Installation Total	Total
Self-Performed									
Remove medicine cabinet	2	L.F.	0.20	0.40		5.90		12	12
Remove vanity top	3	L.F.	0.08	0.24		2.36		7	7
Remove vanity	3	L.F.	0.20	0.60		5.90		18	18
Remove towel bar and tissue dispenser	2	Ea.	0.27	0.54		7.85		16	16
Remove gypsum wallboard ceiling	56	S.F.	0.02	1.12		0.59		33	33
Remove gypsum wallboard	286	S.F.	0.01	2.86		0.24		69	69
Remove existing plumbing partition	24	S.F.	0.01	0.24		0.39		9	9
Remove insulation	20	C.F.	0.01	0.20		0.17		3	3
Remove debris	5	C.Y.	0.67	3.35		19.65		98	98
Frame new plumbing partition	3	L.F.	0.16	0.48	3.69	6.50	11	20	31
Exterior wall insulation	56	S.F.	0.01	0.56	0.30	0.20	17	11	28
Gypsum wallboard ceiling	56	S.F.	0.02	1.12	0.28	0.85	16	48	64
Gypsum wallboard	144	S.F.	0.02	2.88	0.28	0.68	40	98	138
Cementitious backerboard for ceramic tile walls	104	S.F.	0.05	5.20	1.15	1.86	120	193	313
Ceramic tile base	26	L.F.	0.13	3.38	3.45	4.09	90	106	196
Ceramic tile walls	104	S.F.	0.08	8.32	2.30	2.76	239	287	526
Cementitious backerboard for ceramic tile floor	1	S.F.	0.03	0.03	1.15	1.24	1	1	2
Ceramic tile floors	56	S.F.	0.06	3.36	3.45	2.09	193	117	310
Painting, ceiling, walls & door, primer	310	S.F.			0.05	0.14	16	43	59
Painting, ceiling, walls & door, 1 coat	310	S.F.	0.01	3.10	0.05	0.22	16	68	84
Curtain rod, stainless steel, 5' long, 1" diameter	1	Ea.	0.62	0.62	33.50	25	34	25	59
Mirror, plate glass, 30" x 34"	7	S.F.	0.10	0.70	7.10	3.88	50	27	77
Ceramic towel bar and tissue dispenser	1	Ea.	0.20	0.20	10.65	6.40	11	6	17
Trim, baseboard, 9/16" x 3-1/2" wide, pine	12	L.F.	0.03	0.36	1.68	1.36	20	16	36
Subcontract									
Remove combination tub/shower	1	Ea.	1.33	1.33		59		59	59
Pedestal lavatory with supply, waste, & vent	1	Ea.	3.90	3.90	700	156	700	156	856
Bathtub, module/shower wall surround, molded fbgls, 5' long	1	Ea.	4	4	545	159	545	159	704
Fittings for tub & shower	1	Set	7.73	7.73	156	310	156	310	466
Water closet, 2 piece	1	Ea.	3.02	3.02	179	120	179	120	299
Fittings for water closet	1	Set	5.25	5.25	168	209	168	209	377
Electrical, 2 light fixtures with wiring	2	Ea.	0.27	0.54	39.50	11.85	79	24	103
Electrical, 2 light switches	2	Ea.	1.40	2.80	32	62.50	64	125	189
Electrical, one GFI outlet	1	Ea.	1.70	1.70	61.50	75.50	62	76	138
Prefabricated sauna	1	Ea.	23.64	23.64	9000	810	9,000	810	9,810
Dumpster	1	Week	1	1	251	32.50	251	33	284
Subtotals							12,078	3,412	15,490
General Requirements (Site Overhead)						12%	1,449	409	1,859
Subtotals							13,527	3,821	17,349
Overhead and Profit						10%	1,353	382	1,735
Subtotals							14,880	4,203	19,084

Grand Total $19,084

Appendix
& Index

Location Factors

Adjusting Project Costs to Your Location

Costs are based on national averages for materials and installation. To adjust these costs to a specific location, simply multiply the base cost by the factor for that city. The data is arranged alphabetically by state and the first three digits of postal zip code numbers. For a city not listed, use the factor for a nearby city with similar economic characteristics.

STATE	CITY	Residential
ALABAMA		
350-352	Birmingham	.87
354	Tuscaloosa	.73
355	Jasper	.71
356	Decatur	.77
357-358	Huntsville	.84
359	Gadsden	.73
360-361	Montgomery	.76
362	Anniston	.68
363	Dothan	.75
364	Evergreen	.71
365-366	Mobile	.80
367	Selma	.72
368	Phenix City	.73
369	Butler	.71
ALASKA		
995-996	Anchorage	1.26
997	Fairbanks	1.28
998	Juneau	1.26
999	Ketchikan	1.27
ARIZONA		
850,853	Phoenix	.87
852	Mesa/Tempe	.84
855	Globe	.80
856-857	Tucson	.84
859	Show Low	.83
860	Flagstaff	.85
863	Prescott	.82
864	Kingman	.81
865	Chambers	.81
ARKANSAS		
716	Pine Bluff	.75
717	Camden	.65
718	Texarkana	.70
719	Hot Springs	.64
720-722	Little Rock	.81
723	West Memphis	.74
724	Jonesboro	.73
725	Batesville	.71
726	Harrison	.72
727	Fayetteville	.68
728	Russellville	.70
729	Fort Smith	.76
CALIFORNIA		
900-902	Los Angeles	1.06
903-905	Inglewood	1.04
906-908	Long Beach	1.03
910-912	Pasadena	1.04
913-916	Van Nuys	1.07
917-918	Alhambra	1.08
919-921	San Diego	1.04
922	Palm Springs	1.02
923-924	San Bernardino	1.04
925	Riverside	1.06
926-927	Santa Ana	1.04
928	Anaheim	1.07
930	Oxnard	1.07
931	Santa Barbara	1.07
932-933	Bakersfield	1.04

STATE	CITY	Residential
934	San Luis Obispo	1.07
935	Mojave	1.05
936-938	Fresno	1.10
939	Salinas	1.12
940-941	San Francisco	1.21
942,956-958	Sacramento	1.11
943	Palo Alto	1.16
944	San Mateo	1.19
945	Vallejo	1.13
946	Oakland	1.18
947	Berkeley	1.21
948	Richmond	1.22
949	San Rafael	1.20
950	Santa Cruz	1.14
951	San Jose	1.18
952	Stockton	1.09
953	Modesto	1.08
954	Santa Rosa	1.14
955	Eureka	1.09
959	Marysville	1.10
960	Redding	1.10
961	Susanville	1.11
COLORADO		
800-802	Denver	.96
803	Boulder	.94
804	Golden	.92
805	Fort Collins	.91
806	Greeley	.80
807	Fort Morgan	.94
808-809	Colorado Springs	.92
810	Pueblo	.93
811	Alamosa	.90
812	Salida	.91
813	Durango	.93
814	Montrose	.88
815	Grand Junction	.93
816	Glenwood Springs	.92
CONNECTICUT		
060	New Britain	1.06
061	Hartford	1.05
062	Willimantic	1.06
063	New London	1.05
064	Meriden	1.05
065	New Haven	1.06
066	Bridgeport	1.06
067	Waterbury	1.06
068	Norwalk	1.06
069	Stamford	1.07
D.C.		
200-205	Washington	.93
DELAWARE		
197	Newark	1.00
198	Wilmington	1.01
199	Dover	1.00
FLORIDA		
320,322	Jacksonville	.79
321	Daytona Beach	.86
323	Tallahassee	.72

Location Factors

Adjusting Project Costs to Your Location

STATE	CITY	Residential
324	Panama City	.67
325	Pensacola	.75
326,344	Gainesville	.77
327-328,347	Orlando	.85
329	Melbourne	.87
330-332,340	Miami	.83
333	Fort Lauderdale	.84
334,349	West Palm Beach	.84
335-336,346	Tampa	.87
337	St. Petersburg	.77
338	Lakeland	.83
339,341	Fort Myers	.81
342	Sarasota	.85
GEORGIA		
300-303,399	Atlanta	.89
304	Statesboro	.67
305	Gainesville	.74
306	Athens	.74
307	Dalton	.70
308-309	Augusta	.76
310-312	Macon	.78
313-314	Savannah	.79
315	Waycross	.71
316	Valdosta	.71
317	Albany	.75
318-319	Columbus	.80
HAWAII		
967	Hilo	1.22
968	Honolulu	1.23
STATES & POSS.		
969	Guam	1.62
IDAHO		
832	Pocatello	.88
833	Twin Falls	.72
834	Idaho Falls	.72
835	Lewiston	.97
836-837	Boise	.89
838	Coeur d'Alene	.84
ILLINOIS		
600-603	North Suburban	1.09
604	Joliet	1.11
605	South Suburban	1.09
606-608	Chicago	1.15
609	Kankakee	1.00
610-611	Rockford	1.03
612	Rock Island	.96
613	La Salle	1.01
614	Galesburg	.98
615-616	Peoria	1.01
617	Bloomington	.96
618-619	Champaign	.98
620-622	East St. Louis	.97
623	Quincy	.97
624	Effingham	.98
625	Decatur	.97
626-627	Springfield	.98
628	Centralia	.96
629	Carbondale	.96
INDIANA		
460	Anderson	.91
461-462	Indianapolis	.96

STATE	CITY	Residential
463-464	Gary	1.00
465-466	South Bend	.91
467-468	Fort Wayne	.91
469	Kokomo	.92
470	Lawrenceburg	.86
471	New Albany	.85
472	Columbus	.92
473	Muncie	.91
474	Bloomington	.94
475	Washington	.90
476-477	Evansville	.90
478	Terre Haute	.90
479	Lafayette	.91
IOWA		
500-503,509	Des Moines	.92
504	Mason City	.77
505	Fort Dodge	.76
506-507	Waterloo	.80
508	Creston	.81
510-511	Sioux City	.86
512	Sibley	.73
513	Spencer	.75
514	Carroll	.75
515	Council Bluffs	.81
516	Shenandoah	.74
520	Dubuque	.84
521	Decorah	.77
522-524	Cedar Rapids	.93
525	Ottumwa	.83
526	Burlington	.87
527-528	Davenport	.98
KANSAS		
660-662	Kansas City	.95
664-666	Topeka	.79
667	Fort Scott	.85
668	Emporia	.72
669	Belleville	.74
670-672	Wichita	.81
673	Independence	.75
674	Salina	.73
675	Hutchinson	.68
676	Hays	.74
677	Colby	.76
678	Dodge City	.73
679	Liberal	.68
KENTUCKY		
400-402	Louisville	.93
403-405	Lexington	.84
406	Frankfort	.82
407-409	Corbin	.67
410	Covington	.93
411-412	Ashland	.94
413-414	Campton	.68
415-416	Pikeville	.77
417-418	Hazard	.67
420	Paducah	.89
421-422	Bowling Green	.89
423	Owensboro	.82
424	Henderson	.91
425-426	Somerset	.67
427	Elizabethtown	.86
LOUISIANA		
700-701	New Orleans	.85

Location Factors

Adjusting Project Costs to Your Location

STATE	CITY	Residential	STATE	CITY	Residential
703	Thibodaux	.80	553-555	Minneapolis	1.18
704	Hammond	.78	556-558	Duluth	1.10
705	Lafayette	.77	559	Rochester	1.04
706	Lake Charles	.79	560	Mankato	1.00
707-708	Baton Rouge	.78	561	Windom	.84
710-711	Shreveport	.78	562	Willmar	.85
712	Monroe	.73	563	St. Cloud	1.07
713-714	Alexandria	.73	564	Brainerd	.96
			565	Detroit Lakes	.97
MAINE			566	Bemidji	.94
039	Kittery	.80	567	Thief River Falls	.92
040-041	Portland	.88			
042	Lewiston	.88	**MISSISSIPPI**		
043	Augusta	.83	386	Clarksdale	.61
044	Bangor	.86	387	Greenville	.68
045	Bath	.81	388	Tupelo	.64
046	Machias	.82	389	Greenwood	.65
047	Houlton	.86	390-392	Jackson	.73
048	Rockland	.80	393	Meridian	.66
049	Waterville	.75	394	Laurel	.62
			395	Biloxi	.75
MARYLAND			396	McComb	.74
206	Waldorf	.84	397	Columbus	.64
207-208	College Park	.84			
209	Silver Spring	.85	**MISSOURI**		
210-212	Baltimore	.89	630-631	St. Louis	1.01
214	Annapolis	.85	633	Bowling Green	.90
215	Cumberland	.86	634	Hannibal	.87
216	Easton	.68	635	Kirksville	.80
217	Hagerstown	.85	636	Flat River	.93
218	Salisbury	.75	637	Cape Girardeau	.86
219	Elkton	.81	638	Sikeston	.83
			639	Poplar Bluff	.83
MASSACHUSETTS			640-641	Kansas City	1.02
010-011	Springfield	1.05	644-645	St. Joseph	.93
012	Pittsfield	1.02	646	Chillicothe	.85
013	Greenfield	1.01	647	Harrisonville	.94
014	Fitchburg	1.08	648	Joplin	.82
015-016	Worcester	1.11	650-651	Jefferson City	.88
017	Framingham	1.12	652	Columbia	.87
018	Lowell	1.13	653	Sedalia	.85
019	Lawrence	1.12	654-655	Rolla	.88
020-022, 024	Boston	1.19	656-658	Springfield	.84
023	Brockton	1.11			
025	Buzzards Bay	1.10	**MONTANA**		
026	Hyannis	1.09	590-591	Billings	.88
027	New Bedford	1.11	592	Wolf Point	.84
			593	Miles City	.86
MICHIGAN			594	Great Falls	.89
480,483	Royal Oak	1.03	595	Havre	.81
481	Ann Arbor	1.03	596	Helena	.88
482	Detroit	1.10	597	Butte	.83
484-485	Flint	.97	598	Missoula	.83
486	Saginaw	.94	599	Kalispell	.82
487	Bay City	.95			
488-489	Lansing	.96	**NEBRASKA**		
490	Battle Creek	.93	680-681	Omaha	.89
491	Kalamazoo	.92	683-685	Lincoln	.78
492	Jackson	.94	686	Columbus	.69
493,495	Grand Rapids	.83	687	Norfolk	.77
494	Muskegon	.89	688	Grand Island	.77
496	Traverse City	.81	689	Hastings	.76
497	Gaylord	.84	690	Mccook	.69
498-499	Iron Mountain	.90	691	North Platte	.75
			692	Valentine	.66
MINNESOTA			693	Alliance	.65
550-551	Saint Paul	1.13			

Location Factors

Adjusting Project Costs to Your Location

STATE	CITY	Residential		STATE	CITY	Residential
NEVADA				125-126	Poughkeepsie	1.06
889-891	Las Vegas	1.00		127	Monticello	1.03
893	Ely	.90		128	Glens Falls	.88
894-895	Reno	.97		129	Plattsburgh	.92
897	Carson City	.97		130-132	Syracuse	.96
898	Elko	.97		133-135	Utica	.93
				136	Watertown	.91
NEW HAMPSHIRE				137-139	Binghamton	.92
030	Nashua	.90		140-142	Buffalo	1.06
031	Manchester	.90		143	Niagara Falls	1.01
032-033	Concord	.86		144-146	Rochester	.98
034	Keene	.73		147	Jamestown	.88
035	Littleton	.81		148-149	Elmira	.87
036	Charleston	.70				
037	Claremont	.72		**NORTH CAROLINA**		
038	Portsmouth	.84		270,272-274	Greensboro	.73
				271	Winston-Salem	.73
NEW JERSEY				275-276	Raleigh	.74
070-071	Newark	1.12		277	Durham	.73
072	Elizabeth	1.15		278	Rocky Mount	.64
073	Jersey City	1.12		279	Elizabeth City	.61
074-075	Paterson	1.12		280	Gastonia	.74
076	Hackensack	1.11		281-282	Charlotte	.74
077	Long Branch	1.12		283	Fayetteville	.71
078	Dover	1.12		284	Wilmington	.72
079	Summit	1.12		285	Kinston	.62
080,083	Vineland	1.09		286	Hickory	.62
081	Camden	1.10		287-288	Asheville	.72
082,084	Atlantic City	1.13		289	Murphy	.66
085-086	Trenton	1.11				
087	Point Pleasant	1.10		**NORTH DAKOTA**		
088-089	New Brunswick	1.12		580-581	Fargo	.80
				582	Grand Forks	.77
NEW MEXICO				583	Devils Lake	.80
870-872	Albuquerque	.85		584	Jamestown	.75
873	Gallup	.85		585	Bismarck	.80
874	Farmington	.85		586	Dickinson	.77
875	Santa Fe	.85		587	Minot	.80
877	Las Vegas	.85		588	Williston	.77
878	Socorro	.85				
879	Truth/Consequences	.84		**OHIO**		
880	Las Cruces	.83		430-432	Columbus	.96
881	Clovis	.85		433	Marion	.93
882	Roswell	.85		434-436	Toledo	1.01
883	Carrizozo	.85		437-438	Zanesville	.91
884	Tucumcari	.86		439	Steubenville	.96
				440	Lorain	1.01
NEW YORK				441	Cleveland	1.02
100-102	New York	1.36		442-443	Akron	.99
103	Staten Island	1.27		444-445	Youngstown	.96
104	Bronx	1.29		446-447	Canton	.94
105	Mount Vernon	1.15		448-449	Mansfield	.95
106	White Plains	1.19		450	Hamilton	.96
107	Yonkers	1.21		451-452	Cincinnati	.96
108	New Rochelle	1.21		453-454	Dayton	.92
109	Suffern	1.13		455	Springfield	.94
110	Queens	1.27		456	Chillicothe	.96
111	Long Island City	1.30		457	Athens	.90
112	Brooklyn	1.32		458	Lima	.92
113	Flushing	1.29				
114	Jamaica	1.29		**OKLAHOMA**		
115,117,118	Hicksville	1.19		730-731	Oklahoma City	.80
116	Far Rockaway	1.28		734	Ardmore	.78
119	Riverhead	1.20		735	Lawton	.81
120-122	Albany	.95		736	Clinton	.77
123	Schenectady	.96		737	Enid	.77
124	Kingston	1.02		738	Woodward	.76

Location Factors

Adjusting Project Costs to Your Location

STATE	CITY	Residential
739	Guymon	.67
740-741	Tulsa	.79
743	Miami	.82
744	Muskogee	.72
745	Mcalester	.74
746	Ponca City	.77
747	Durant	.76
748	Shawnee	.76
749	Poteau	.77
OREGON		
970-972	Portland	1.02
973	Salem	1.01
974	Eugene	1.01
975	Medford	.99
976	Klamath Falls	1.00
977	Bend	1.02
978	Pendleton	.99
979	Vale	.99
PENNSYLVANIA		
150-152	Pittsburgh	.99
153	Washington	.94
154	Uniontown	.91
155	Bedford	.89
156	Greensburg	.95
157	Indiana	.91
158	Dubois	.90
159	Johnstown	.90
160	Butler	.93
161	New Castle	.93
162	Kittanning	.94
163	Oil City	.89
164-165	Erie	.97
166	Altoona	.89
167	Bradford	.89
168	State College	.92
169	Wellsboro	.88
170-171	Harrisburg	.94
172	Chambersburg	.89
173-174	York	.88
175-176	Lancaster	.91
177	Williamsport	85
178	Sunbury	.89
179	Pottsville	.89
180	Lehigh Valley	.98
181	Allentown	1.01
182	Hazleton	.89
183	Stroudsburg	.92
184-185	Scranton	.95
186-187	Wilkes-Barre	.91
188	Montrose	.89
189	Doylestown	1.04
190-191	Philadelphia	1.14
193	Westchester	1.07
194	Norristown	1.03
195-196	Reading	.96
PUERTO RICO		
009	San Juan	.84
RHODE ISLAND		
028	Newport	1.08
029	Providence	1.08
SOUTH CAROLINA		
290-292	Columbia	.73

STATE	CITY	Residential
293	Spartanburg	.71
294	Charleston	.72
295	Florence	.66
296	Greenville	.70
297	Rock Hill	.65
298	Aiken	.83
299	Beaufort	.67
SOUTH DAKOTA		
570-571	Sioux Falls	.77
572	Watertown	.73
573	Mitchell	.75
574	Aberdeen	.76
575	Pierre	.76
576	Mobridge	.73
577	Rapid City	.76
TENNESSEE		
370-372	Nashville	.85
373-374	Chattanooga	.77
375,380-381	Memphis	.85
376	Johnson City	.72
377-379	Knoxville	.75
382	Mckenzie	.70
383	Jackson	.71
384	Columbia	.72
385	Cookeville	.68
TEXAS		
750	Mckinney	.75
751	Waxahachie	.76
752-753	Dallas	.83
754	Greenville	.69
755	Texarkana	.74
756	Longview	.68
757	Tyler	.74
758	Palestine	.67
759	Lufkin	.72
760-761	Fort Worth	.83
762	Denton	.77
763	Wichita Falls	.79
764	Eastland	.72
765	Temple	.75
766-767	Waco	.77
768	Brownwood	.68
769	San Angelo	.72
770-772	Houston	.85
773	Huntsville	.69
774	Wharton	.70
775	Galveston	.83
776-777	Beaumont	.82
778	Bryan	.74
779	Victoria	.74
780	Laredo	.73
781-782	San Antonio	.80
783-784	Corpus Christi	.77
785	Mc Allen	.75
786-787	Austin	.79
788	Del Rio	.66
789	Giddings	.70
790-791	Amarillo	.78
792	Childress	.76
793-794	Lubbock	.76
795-796	Abilene	.75
797	Midland	.76
798-799,885	El Paso	.75

Location Factors

Adjusting Project Costs to Your Location

STATE	CITY	Residential
UTAH		
840-841	Salt Lake City	.83
842,844	Ogden	.81
843	Logan	.82
845	Price	.72
846-847	Provo	.83
VERMONT		
050	White River Jct.	.73
051	Bellows Falls	.75
052	Bennington	.74
053	Brattleboro	.75
054	Burlington	.80
056	Montpelier	.82
057	Rutland	.81
058	St. Johnsbury	.75
059	Guildhall	.74
VIRGINIA		
220-221	Fairfax	.85
222	Arlington	.87
223	Alexandria	.90
224-225	Fredericksburg	.75
226	Winchester	.71
227	Culpeper	.77
228	Harrisonburg	.67
229	Charlottesville	.72
230-232	Richmond	.81
233-235	Norfolk	.81
236	Newport News	.79
237	Portsmouth	.77
238	Petersburg	.78
239	Farmville	.68
240-241	Roanoke	.72
242	Bristol	.67
243	Pulaski	.66
244	Staunton	.68
245	Lynchburg	.69
246	Grundy	.67
WASHINGTON		
980-981,987	Seattle	1.01
982	Everett	1.03
983-984	Tacoma	1.00
985	Olympia	1.00
986	Vancouver	.97
988	Wenatchee	.90
989	Yakima	.95
990-992	Spokane	1.00
993	Richland	.97
994	Clarkston	.96
WEST VIRGINIA		
247-248	Bluefield	.88
249	Lewisburg	.89
250-253	Charleston	.97
254	Martinsburg	.84
255-257	Huntington	.96
258-259	Beckley	.90
260	Wheeling	.92
261	Parkersburg	.91
262	Buckhannon	.91
263-264	Clarksburg	.90
265	Morgantown	.91
266	Gassaway	.92
267	Romney	.86
268	Petersburg	.88

STATE	CITY	Residential
WISCONSIN		
530,532	Milwaukee	1.05
531	Kenosha	1.03
534	Racine	1.01
535	Beloit	.99
537	Madison	.99
538	Lancaster	.97
539	Portage	.96
540	New Richmond	.98
541-543	Green Bay	1.01
544	Wausau	.95
545	Rhinelander	.95
546	La Crosse	.94
547	Eau Claire	.98
548	Superior	.97
549	Oshkosh	.95
WYOMING		
820	Cheyenne	.75
821	Yellowstone Nat. Pk.	.70
822	Wheatland	.71
823	Rawlins	.69
824	Worland	.69
825	Riverton	.70
826	Casper	.76
827	Newcastle	.68
828	Sheridan	.73
829-831	Rock Springs	.73
ALBERTA		
	Calgary	1.06
	Edmonton	1.05
	Fort McMurray	1.03
	Lethbridge	1.04
	Lloydminster	1.03
	Medicine Hat	1.04
	Red Deer	1.04
BRITISH COLUMBIA		
	Kamloops	1.01
	Prince George	1.01
	Vancouver	1.08
	Victoria	1.01
MANITOBA		
	Brandon	1.00
	Portage la Prairie	1.00
	Winnipeg	1.01
NEW BRUNSWICK		
	Bathurst	.91
	Dalhousie	.91
	Fredericton	.99
	Moncton	.91
	Newcastle	.91
	Saint John	.99
NEWFOUNDLAND		
	Corner Brook	.92
	St. John's	.93
NORTHWEST TERRITORIES		
	Yellowknife	.98

Location Factors

Adjusting Project Costs to Your Location

STATE	CITY	Residential
NOVA SCOTIA		
	Dartmouth	.93
	Halifax	.93
	New Glasgow	.93
	Sydney	.91
	Yarmouth	.93
ONTARIO		
	Barrie	1.10
	Brantford	1.12
	Cornwall	1.11
	Hamilton	1.12
	Kingston	1.11
	Kitchener	1.06
	London	1.10
	North Bay	1.08
	Oshawa	1.10
	Ottawa	1.12
	Owen Sound	1.09
	Peterborough	1.09
	Sarnia	1.12
	Sudbury	1.03
	Thunder Bay	1.08
	Toronto	1.15
	Windsor	1.09
PRINCE EDWARD ISLAND		
	Charlottetown	.88
	Summerside	.88
QUEBEC		
	Cap-de-la-Madeleine	1.11
	Charlesbourg	1.11
	Chicoutimi	1.11
	Gatineau	1.10
	Laval	1.11
	Montreal	1.11
	Quebec	1.13
	Sherbrooke	1.10
	Trois Rivieres	1.11
SASKATCHEWAN		
	Moose Jaw	.91
	Prince Albert	.90
	Regina	.92
	Saskatoon	.91
YUKON		
	Whitehorse	.90

Safety Tips

Safety is an essential component of a successful contracting business. You need to know your legal responsibilities regarding safety, make sure your employees are properly trained, and conduct your jobs safely. Many legal contracts with the homeowner state that the contractor is responsible for safety on the site. Controlling the cost of your insurance premiums also means making safety a priority.

The following tips are not intended as a complete list, but pertain to common situations in residential remodeling.

- **Protect yourself:** Wear the proper clothing and gear to protect yourself from possible hazards. Avoid loose or torn clothes, especially when working with power tools. Wear heavy shoes or boots, safety glasses when working with power tools, a hardhat if materials or tools could fall on your head, and work gloves when possible. Use hearing protection when operating loud machinery or when hammering in a small, enclosed space. Wear a dust mask to keep from inhaling sawdust, insulation fibers, or other airborne particles.

- **Organize the work area:** Make a point of keeping your work space neat and organized. Eliminate tripping hazards and clutter, especially in areas used for access. Take the time to clean up and reorganize as you go. This will not only make for a safer work area, but will help you be more productive over the long run. Increases in productivity have a direct relationship to increases in the bottom line.

- **Do not strain yourself:** When lifting equipment or materials, always try to let your leg muscles do the work, not your back. Seek assistance when moving heavy or awkward objects, and, remember, if an object is on wheels, it is easier to push than to pull it.

- **Check equipment for safety:** When working from a ladder, scaffold, or temporary platform, make sure it is stable and well-braced. Keep stepladders in new or like new condition. Inspect staging planks frequently for signs of wear. Double check fall protection equipment and barricades before and after use. Replace defective equipment immediately.

- **Follow product manufacturers' recommendations:** When working with adhesives, protective coatings, or other volatile products, be sure to follow their installation and ventilation guidelines. Pay particular attention to drying times and fire hazards associated with the product. If possible, obtain from the supplier a Material Safety Data Sheet, which will clearly describe any associated hazards.

- **Shut off affected utilities:** When working with electricity or gas, be sure you know how to shut off the supply when needed. It may be wise to invest in a simple current-testing device to determine when electric current is present. If you don't already have one, purchase a fire extinguisher, learn how to use it, and keep it handy.

- **Use tools correctly:** Keep in mind that you'll need special tools for some jobs. Study how to use them, and practice with them before undertaking final moves on your project. When using power tools, never pin back safety guards. Choose the correct cutting blade for the material you are using. Keep children or bystanders away from the work area, and never interrupt someone using a power tool or actively performing an operation. Keep drill bits, blades, and cutters sharp; dull tools require extra force and can be dangerous. Always unplug tools when leaving them unattended or when servicing or changing blades.

A few tips on hand tools:

- Do not use any tool for a purpose other than the one for which it was designed. In other words, do not use a screwdriver as a pry bar, pliers as a hammer, etc.

- Do not use any striking tool (such as a hammer or sledgehammer) that has dents or cracks, shows excessive wear, or has a damaged or loose handle. Also, do not strike a hammer with another hammer in an attempt to remove a stubborn nail, get at an awkward spot, etc. Do not strike hard objects (such as concrete or steel), which could chip the tool and cause personal injury.

Resources

The following list of product manufacturers is provided as a starting point for gathering project information. It is not intended to be all-inclusive or an endorsement of any particular products.

Products

Accessible Bath Fixtures:

Accessible Environments, Inc.
P.O. Box 2208
Gloucester, VA 23601
800-643-5906
www.accessinc.com

Bathease, Inc.
3815 Darston Street
Palm Harbor, FL 34685
888-747-7845
www.bathease.com

Dunleavy-Cordun Associates, Inc.
1260 Caledonia Road
Toronto, ON M6A 2X5
Canada
877-737-3633
www.dunleavycordun.com

LASCO Bathware
8101 E. Kaiser Boulevard
Suite 130
Anaheim, CA 92808
800-877-2005
www.lascobathware.com

Rohl
1559 Sunland Lane
Costa Mesa, CA 92626
714-557-1933
www.rohlhome.com

Appliances:

Amana
Maytag
403 W. 4th Street, N.
Newton, IA 50208
800-843-0304
www.amana.com

Asko
AM Appliance Group
P.O. Box 851805
Richardson, TX 75085
972-644-8595
www.askousa.com

Bosch
BSH Home Appliances Corporation
5551 McFadden Avenue
Huntington Beach, CA 92649
800-921-9622
www.boschappliances.com

Elmira Stove Works
232 Arthur Street, S.
Elmira, ON N3B 2P2
Canada
800-295-8498
www.elmirastoveworks.com

Gaggenau
BSH Home Appliances Corporation
5551 McFadden Avenue
Huntington Beach, CA 92649
800-828-9165
www.gaggenau.com

General Electric
800-626-2005
www.geappliances.com

Haier
877-337-3639
www.haieramerica.com

Insinkerator
800-558-5700
www.insinkerator.com

Jenn-Air
240 Edwards Street
Cleveland, TN 37311
800-688-1100
www.jennair.com

Kenmore
Sears
3333 Beverly Road
Hoffman Estates, IL 60179
800-349-4358
www.sears.com/kenmore

Kitchen-Aid
P.O. Box 218
St. Joseph, MI 49085
800-422-1230
www.kitchenaid.com

Maytag
240 Edwards Street
Cleveland, TN 37311
800-688-9900
www.maytag.com

Miele
9 Independence Way
Princeton, NJ 08540
800-843-7231
www.miele.com

Sub-Zero
P.O. Box 44130
Madison, WI 53744
800-222-7820
www.subzero.com

Thermador
5551 McFadden Avenue
Huntington Beach, CA 92649
800-656-9226
www.thermador.com

Viking
111 Front Street
Greenwood, MS 38930
662-455-1200
www.vikingrange.com

Whirlpool Corporation
800-253-1301
www.whirlpool.com

Wolf Appliance Company, LLC
P.O. Box 44848
Madison, WI 53744
800-332-9513
www.wolfappliance.com

Bath & Kitchen Sinks/ Lavatories, Fittings, & Accessories:

American Standard
P.O. Box 6820
1 Centennial Plaza
Piscataway, NJ 08855
800-442-1902
www.americanstandard.com

Blanco America, Inc.
110 Mount Holly By-Pass
Lumberton, NJ 08048
www.blancoamerica.com

Delta Faucet Company
55 E. 111th Street
P.O. Box 40980
Indianapolis, IN 46280
800-345-3358
www.deltafaucet.com

Eljer
14801 Quorum Drive
Dallas, TX 75254
800-423-5537
www.eljer.com

Elkay
2222 Camden Court
Oak Brook, IL 60523
630-574-8484
www.elkayusa.com

Grohe America Inc.
241 Covington Drive
Bloomingdale, IL 60108
800-444-7643
www.groheamerica.com

Jacuzzi Whirlpool Bath
14801 Quorum Drive
Suite 550
Dallas, TX 75254
800-288-4002
www.jacuzzi.com

Karran Plumbing Products
1422 East Elkhorn Road
Vincennes, IN 47591
866-452 7726
www.karranproducts.com

Kohler
444 Highland Drive
Kohler, WI 53044
800-456-4537
www.kohler.com

Majestic Shower Company
1795 Yosemite Avenue
San Francisco, CA 94124
800-675-6225
www.majesticshower.com

Moen
800-289-6636
www.moen.com

MrSauna, Sussman Lifestyle Group
43-20 34th Street
Long Island City, NY 11101
800-767-8326
www.mrsauna.com

MrSteam
43-20 34th Street
Long Island City, NY 11101
800-767-8326
www.mrsteam.com

Ondine (of Interbath, Inc.) Luxury Shower Systems
665 N. Baldwin Park Boulevard
City of Industry, CA 91746
800-423-9485
www.interbath.com/ondine

Robern Bathroom Products
701 N. Wilson Avenue
Bristol, PA 19007
800-877-2376
www.robern.com

Saunatec
575 E. Cokato Street
Cokato, MN 55321
888-780-4427
www.saunatec.com

Sterling Plumbing
888-783-7546
www.sterlingplumbing.com

Toto Toilets and Bidets
1155 Southern Road
Morrow, GA 30260
888-295-8134
www.totousa.com

Ultra Baths
956 Chemin Olivier
Saint-Nicolas, Québec G7A 2N1
Canada
800-463-2187
www.ultrabaths.com

Warmatowel, Inc.
www.warmatowel.com

Waterworks
800-998-2284
www.waterworks.com

Westendorf Plastics, Inc.
14310 "C" Circle
Omaha, NE 68144
800-747-0500
www.whirlpooltubs.com

Cabinets:

Crystal Cabinet Works, Inc.
100 Crystal Drive
Princeton, MN 55371
800-347-5045
www.ccworks.com

Fieldstone Cabinetry
600 E. 48th Street, N.
Sioux Falls, SD 57104
800-339-5369
www.fieldstonecabinetry.com

KraftMaid Cabinetry
P.O. Box 1055
Middlefield, OH 44062
440-632-5333
www.kraftmaid.com

Merillat Industries
800-575-8763
www.merillat.com

StarMark Cabinetry
600 E. 48th Street, N.
Sioux Falls, SD 57104
800-594-9444
www.starmarkcabinetry.com

Thomasville Cabinets
800-756-6497
www.thomasvillecabinetry.com

Wellborn Cabinet, Inc.
P.O. Box 1210
Ashland, AL 36251
800-336-8040
www.wellborn.com

Wood-Mode
570-374-2711
www.wood-mode.com

Ceiling Fans:

Casablanca
761 Corporate Center Drive
Pomona, CA 91768
888-227-2178
www.casablancafanco.com

Hunter Fan Company
2500 Frisco Avenue
Memphis, TN 38114
888-830-1326
www.hunterfan.com

Countertops:

Cambria
866-226-2742
www.cambriausa.com

Chemetal—Stainless Countertops and Backsplashes
39 O'Neill Street
Easthampton, MA 01027
800-807-7341
www.chemetalco.com

Corian
DuPont Building
1007 Market Street
Wilmington, DE 19898
800-426-7426
www.corian.com

Formica Corporation
255 E. 5th Street
Suite 200
Cincinnati, OH 45202
800-367-6422
www.formica.com

LG Solid Source, LLC
8009 W. Olive
Peoria, AZ 85345
877-853-1805
www.lghi-macs.com

Silestone
Cosentino USA
13124 Trinity Drive
Stafford, TX 77477
800-291-1311
www.silestoneusa.com
www.ecounters.com

Sonoma Cast Stone
P.O. Box 1721
Sonoma, CA 95476
888-807-4234
www.sonomastone.com

Volcanics (solid surface countertops)
8009 W. Olive
Peoria, AZ 85345
877-853-1805
www.lgvolcanics.com

Wilsonart International
2400 Wilson Place
P.O. Box 6110
Temple, TX 76503
800-433-3222
www.wilsonart.com

Fireplaces:

Travis Industries
Fireplace Xtrordinair
4800 Harbour Point Boulevard, S.W.
Mukilteo, WA 98275
800-654-1177
www.fireplacextrordinair.com

Flooring:

Concrete, Stone, and Tile:

Allied Tile Manufacturing Corp.
2840 Atlantic Avenue
Brooklyn, NY 11207
800-827-5457
www.alliedtile.com

American Olean Tile
www.aotile.com

Ann Sacks Tile & Stone
800-278-8453
www.annsacks.com

Artistic Tile
800-260-8646
www.artistictile.com

Dal-Tile
7834 C.F. Hawn Freeway
Dallas, TX 75217
214-398-1411
www.daltile.com

Diamond D Concrete
310 D Kennedy Drive
Capitola, CA 95010
831-464-7369
www.diamonddcompany.com

Florida Tile
P.O. Box 447
Lakeland, FL 33802
863-284-4156
www.floridatile.com

Limestone Concept, Inc.
P.O. Box 352026
Los Angeles, CA 90035
310-278-9829
www.limestoneconcept.com

The Stoneyard
2 Spectacle Pond Road
Littleton, MA 01460
800-231-2200
www.stoneyard.com

Summitville Tiles
330-223-1511
www.summitville.com

Laminate:

Pergo Floors
3128 Highwoods Boulevard
Raleigh, NC 27604
800-337-3746
www.pergo.com

Witex laminate flooring
800-948-3987
www.witexusa.com

Resilient:

The Amtico Studio
6480 Roswell Road
Atlanta, GA 30328
404-267-1900
www.amtico.com

Armstrong World Industries
P.O. Box 3001
Lancaster, PA 17604
800-233-3823
www.armstrong.com

Congoleum Corporation
Department C
P.O. Box 3127
Mercerville, NJ 08619
800-274-3266
www.congoleum.com

Domco Sheet Flooring
1001 Yamaska, E.
Farnham, Quebec J2N 1J7
Canada
800-367-8275
www.domco.com

Forbo Marmolean
P.O. Box 667
Humboldt Industrial Park
Hazleton, PA 18201
570-459-0771
www.themarmoleumstore.com

Mannington Resilient Floors
75 Mannington Mills Road
Salem, NJ 08079
856-935-3000
www.mannington.com

Metroflor Vinyl Flooring
15 Oakwood Avenue
Norwalk, CT 06850
203-299-3100
www.metroflorusa.com

Nova Linoleum
1710 E. Sepulveda Boulevard
Carson, CA 90745
866-576-2458
www.novafloorings.com

Wood:

Bruce Hardwood
P.O. Box 3001
Lancaster, PA 17604
800-233-3823
www.armstrong.com/resbrucewoodna

Expanko Cork Flooring
3135 Lower Valley Road
Parkesburg, PA 19365
800-345-6202
www.expanko.com

Harris Tarkett Wood Floors
2225 Eddie Williams Road
Johnson City, TN 37601
423-979-3700
www.harris-tarkett.com

Lumber Liquidators
3000 John Deere Road
Toano, VA 23168
800-476-0007
www.lumberliquidators.com

Mohawk floors
www.mohawk-hardwoodflooring.com

Oshkosh Floor Designs
911 E. Main Street
Winneconne, WI 54986
877-582-9977
www.oshkoshfloors.com

Wide Plank International
Reclaimed Wood Flooring
427 E. 90 Street
New York, NY10128
212-426-7505
www.wideplank.com

Lighting:

Cooper Lighting
1121 Highway 74, S.
Peachtree City, GA 30269
770-486-4800
www.cooperlighting.com

Hudson Valley Lighting, Inc.
P.O. Box 7459
Newburgh, NY 12550
845-561-0300
www.hudsonvalleylighting.com

Leviton
59-25 Little Neck Parkway
Little Neck, NY 11362
718-229-4040
www.leviton.com

Lightolier
631 Airport Road
Fall River, MA 02720
508-679-8131
www.lightolier.com

Lutron Electronics Company, Inc.
7200 Suter Road
Coopersburg, PA 18036
888-588-7661
www.lutron.com

Moldings:

Balmer Architectural Moldings
271 Yorkland Boulevard
Toronto, ON M2J 1S5
Canada
800-665-3454
www.balmer.com

Birger Juell Ltd.
150 Merchandise Mart Place
Chicago, IL 60654
312-464-9663
www.birgerjuell.com

Hull Historical Millwork
201 Lipscomb Street
Fort Worth, TX 76104
817-332-1495
www.hullhistorical.com

Fypon Decorative Moldings
800-446-3040
www.fypon.com

ResinArt Plastic Moldings
201 Old Airport Road
Fletcher, NC 28732
800-497-4376
www.flexmoulding.com

Paint:

BEHR
3400 W. Segerstrom Avenue
Santa Ana, CA 92704
800-854-0133
www.behr.com

Benjamin Moore
51 Chestnut Ridge Road
Montvale, NJ 07645
800-344-0400
www.benjaminmoore.com

Sherwin Williams
www.sherwin-williams.com

Ventilation:

Broan Ventilation
P.O. Box 140
Hartford, WI 53027
800-558-1711

NuTone
888-336-3948
www.nutone.com

Vent-A-Hood
P.O. Box 830426
Richardson, TX 75083
800-331-2493
www.ventahood.com

Zephyr Corporation
395 Mendell Street
San Francisco, CA 94124
888-880-8368
www.zephyronline.com

Windows, Doors, Skylights, & Solar Energy Systems:

Andersen Corporation
100 Fourth Avenue, N.
Bayport, MN 55003
651-264-5150
www.andersencorp.com

Marvin Windows and Doors
P.O. Box 100
Warroad, MN 56763
888-537-7828
www.marvin.com

Peachtree Doors and Windows
888 Southview Drive
Mosinee, WI 54455
888-888-3814
www.peach99.com

Pella Windows and Doors
102 Main Street
Pella, IA 50219
www.pella.com

Velux
800-888-3589
www.velux.com

Weather Shield Windows
1 Weather Shield Plaza
P.O. Box 309
Medford, WI 54451
800-447-6808
www.weathershield.com

Additional Information

American National Standards Institute (ANSI)
1819 L Street, N.W.
6th Floor
Washington, DC 20036
202-293-8020
www.ansi.org

American Society of Heating, Refrigeration, and Air Conditioning Engineers (ASHRAE)
1791 Tullie Circle, N.E.
Atlanta, GA 30329
800-527-4723
www.ashrae.org

Americans with Disabilities Act (ADA)
U.S. Department of Justice
950 Pennsylvania Avenue, N.W.
Civil Rights Division
Disability Rights Section - NYAV
Washington, DC 20530
800-514-0301
www.ada.gov

Association of the Wall and Ceiling Industries (AWCI)
803 W. Broad Street
Suite 600
Falls Church, VA 22046
703-534-8300
www.awci.org

Ceramic Tile Institute of America
12061 Jefferson Boulevard
Culver City, CA 90230
800-356-9993
www.ctioa.org

ConcreteNetwork.com
Residential concrete information, products, and service providers.
www.concretenetwork.com

ENERGYSTAR®
United States Environmental Protection Agency Climate Protection Partnerships Division
1200 Pennsylvania Avenue, N.W.
Washington, DC 20460
888-782-7937
www.energystar.gov

Institute of Electrical and Electronic Engineers (IEEE)
1828 L Street, N.W.
Suite 1202
Washington, DC 20036
202-785-0017
www.ieee.org

International Association of Plumbing and Mechanical Officials (IAPMO)
5001 E. Philadelphia Street
Ontario, CA 91761
USA
909-472-4100
www.iapmo.org

Kitchen Cabinet Manufacturers Association
1899 Preston White Drive
Reston, VA 20191
703-264-1690
www.kcma.org

Marble Institute of America
28901 Clemens Road
Suite 100
Westlake, OH 44145
440-250-9222
www.marble-institute.com

Masonry Institute of America
386 Beech Avenue, #4
Torrance, CA 90501
310-328-4400
www.masonryinstitute.org

National Association of Home Builders
(NAHB)
1201 15th Street, N.W.
Washington, DC 20005
800-368-5242
www.nahb.org

National Association of the Remodeling
Industry (NARI)
780 Lee Street
Suite 200
Des Plaines, IL 60016
800-611-6274
www.nari.org

National Electrical Contractors
Association (NECA)
3 Bethesda Metro Center
Suite 1100
Bethesda, MD 20814
301-657-3110
www.necanet.org

National Kitchen & Bath Association
(NKBA)
687 Willow Grove Street
Hackettstown, NJ 07840
800-843-6522
www.nkba.org

Painting & Decorating Contractors of
America
11960 Westline Industrial Drive
Suite 201
St. Louis, MO 63146
800-332-7322
www.pdca.org

Professional Remodeler Magazine
www.housingzone.com/pr

Tile Council of America
100 Clemson Research Boulevard
Anderson, SC 29625
864-646-8453
www.tileusa.com

U.S. Consumer Product Safety
Commission (CPSC)
Washington, DC 20207
800-638-2772

Pool and spa safety publications
www.cpsc.gov/cpscpub/pubs/
chdrown.html

Bibliography

Basics: Home Renovation, by Ela Schwartz, Barnes & Noble, 2004.

Baths: Your Guide to Planning & Remodeling, Better Homes and Gardens Books, 1996.

Builder's Essentials: Best Business Practices for Builders & Remodelers, by Thomas Frisby, RSMeans, 2001.

Contractor's Pricing Guide: Residential Detailed Costs, 11th ed., RSMeans, 2005.

Contractor's Pricing Guide: Residential Repair & Remodeling, 5th ed., RSMeans, 2005.

Means Illustrated Construction Dictionary, Unabridged 3rd ed., RSMeans, 2000.

Interior Home Improvement Cost Guide, 9th ed., RSMeans, 2004.

Kitchen Trends Magazine, Trends Publishing USA, Inc.

Kitchens: Your Guide to Planning & Remodeling, Better Homes and Gardens Books, 1996.

National Association of Home Builders Remodelor's Council. Text excerpt from a course titled, "Working with and Marketing to Older Adults," one of the requirements for earning the Certified Aging-in-Place Specialist (CAPS) designation.

National Association of Home Builders University of Housing. Text excerpt from a course titled, "Sales and Marketing for Remodelers," one of the requirements for the Certified Graduate Remodelor (CGR) designation. For more information on NAHB, visit their Web site at www.nahb.org/designations or call the Designation Help Line at 800-368-5242 ext. 8154.

Remodeler's Instant Answers, by R. Dodge Woodson, McGraw-Hill, 2004.

Repair & Remodeling Estimating Methods, 4th ed., by Edward Wetherill and Merl Vandervort, RSMeans, 2002.

The New Smart Approach to Bath Design, Susan Maney, Creative Homeowner Press, 2003.

This Old House Magazine, Special Edition, Kitchen & Bath, April 2005. This Old House Ventures, Inc.

Reed Construction Data, Inc.

Reed Construction Data, Inc., a leading worldwide provider of total construction information solutions, is comprised of three main product groups designed specifically to help construction professionals advance their businesses with timely, accurate and actionable project, product, and cost data. Reed Construction Data is a division of Reed Business Information, a member of the Reed Elsevier plc group of companies.

The *Project, Product, and Cost & Estimating* divisions offer a variety of innovative products and services designed for the full spectrum of design, construction, and manufacturing professionals. Through it's *International* companies, Reed Construction Data's reputation for quality construction market data is growing worldwide.

Cost Information
RSMeans, the undisputed market leader and authority on construction costs, publishes current cost and estimating information in annual cost books and on the CostWorks CD-ROM. RSMeans furnishes the construction industry with a rich library of complementary reference books and a series of professional seminars that are designed to sharpen professional skills and maximize the effective use of cost estimating and management tools. RSMeans also provides construction cost consulting for Owners, Manufacturers, Designers, and Contractors.

Project Data
Reed Construction Data provides complete, accurate and relevant project information through all stages of construction. Customers are supplied industry data through leads, project reports, contact lists, plans and specifications surveys, market penetration analyses and sales evaluation reports. Any of these products can pinpoint a county, look at a state, or cover the country. Data is delivered via paper, e-mail, CD-ROM or the Internet.

Building Product Information
The First Source suite of products is the only integrated building product information system offered to the commercial construction industry for comparing and specifying building products. These print and online resources include *First Source*, CSI's SPEC-DATA™, CSI's MANU-SPEC™, First Source CAD, and Manufacturer Catalogs. Written by industry professionals and organized using CSI's MasterFormat™, construction professionals use this information to make better design decisions.

FirstSourceONL.com combines Reed Construction Data's project, product and cost data with news and information from Reed Business Information's *Building Design & Construction* and *Consulting-Specifying Engineer,* this industry-focused site offers easy and unlimited access to vital information for all construction professionals.

International
BIMSA/Mexico provides construction project news, product information, cost-data, seminars and consulting services to construction professionals in Mexico. Its subsidiary, PRISMA, provides job costing software.

Byggfakta Scandinavia AB, founded in 1936, is the parent company for the leaders of customized construction market data for Denmark, Estonia, Finland, Norway and Sweden. Each company fully covers the local construction market and provides information across several platforms including subscription, ad-hoc basis, electronically and on paper.

Reed Construction Data Canada serves the Canadian construction market with reliable and comprehensive project and product information services that cover all facets of construction. Core services include: *BuildSource, BuildSpec, BuildSelect,* product selection and specification tools available in print and on the Internet; Building Reports, a national construction project lead service; CanaData, statistical and forecasting information; *Daily Commercial News,* a construction newspaper reporting on news and projects in Ontario; and *Journal of Commerce,* reporting news in British Columbia and Alberta.

Cordell Building Information Services, with its complete range of project and cost and estimating services, is Australia's specialist in the construction information industry. Cordell provides in-depth and historical information on all aspects of construction projects and estimation, including several customized reports, construction and sales leads, and detailed cost information among others.

For more information, please visit our Web site at www.reedconstructiondata.com.

Reed Construction Data, Inc., Corporate Office
30 Technology Parkway South
Norcross, GA 30092-2912
(800) 322-6996
(800) 895-8661 (fax)
info@reedbusiness.com
www.reedconstructiondata.com

Contractor's Pricing Guides

For more information
visit Means Web Site
at www.rsmeans.com

Contractor's Pricing Guide:
Residential Detailed Costs 2005

Every aspect of residential construction, from overhead costs to residential lighting and wiring, is in here. All the detail you need to accurately estimate the costs of your work with or without markups–labor-hours, typical crews and equipment are included as well. When you need a detailed estimate, this publication has all the costs to help you come up with a complete, on the money, price you can rely on to win profitable work.

$39.95 per copy
Over 350 pages, with charts and tables, 8-1/2 x 11
Catalog No. 60335   ISBN 0-87629-762-9

Contractor's Pricing Guide:
Residential Repair & Remodeling Costs 2005

This book provides total unit price costs for every aspect of the most common repair & remodeling projects. Organized in the order of construction by component and activity, it includes demolition and installation, cleaning, painting, and more.

With simplified estimating methods; clear, concise descriptions; and technical specifications for each component, the book is a valuable tool for contractors who want to speed up their estimating time, while making sure their costs are on target.

$39.95 per copy
Over 300 pages, illustrated, 8-1/2 x 11
Catalog No. 60345   ISBN 0-87629-761-0

Contractor's Pricing Guide:
Residential Square Foot Costs 2005

Now available in one concise volume, all you need to know to plan and budget the cost of new homes. If you are looking for a quick reference, the model home section contains costs for over 250 different sizes and types of residences, with hundreds of easily applied modifications. If you need even more detail, the Assemblies Section lets you build your own costs or modify the model costs further. Hundreds of graphics are provided, along with forms and procedures to help you get it right.

$39.95 per copy
Over 300 pages, illustrated, 8-1/2 x 11
Catalog No. 60325   ISBN 0-87629-763-7

Plumbing Estimating Methods
New 3rd Edition
By Joseph Galeno and Sheldon Greene

This newly updated, practical guide walks you through a complete plumbing estimate, from basic materials and installation methods through to change order analysis. It contains everything needed for plumbing estimating and covers:

- Residential, commercial, industrial, and medical systems
- Updated, expanded information using *Means Plumbing Cost Data*
- Sample takeoff and estimate forms
- Detailed illustrations of systems & components

$59.95 per copy
Over 330 pages
Catalog No. 67283B   ISBN 0-87629-704-1

Green Building: Project Planning & Cost Estimating
By RSMeans and Contributing Authors

Written by a team of leading experts in sustainable design, this is a complete guide to planning and estimating green building projects, a growing trend in building design and construction. It explains:

- How to select and specify green products
- How the project team works differently on a green versus a traditional building project
- What criteria your building needs to meet to get a LEED, Energy Star, or other recognized rating for green buildings

Features an extensive Green Building Cost Data section, which details the available products, how they are specified, and how much they cost.

$89.95 per copy
350 pages, illustrated, hardcover
Catalog No. 67338   ISBN 0-87629-659-2

Residential & Light Commercial Construction Standards, 2nd Edition
By RSMeans and Contributing Authors

New, updated second edition of this unique collection of industry standards that define quality construction. For contractors, subcontractors, owners, developers, architects, engineers, attorneys, and insurance personnel, this book provides authoritative requirements and recommendations compiled from the nation's leading professional associations, industry publications, and building code organizations.

$59.95 per copy
600 pages, illustrated, softcover
Catalog No. 67322A   ISBN 0-87629-658-4

Books for Builders

For more information
visit Means Web Site
at www.rsmeans.com

Builder's Essentials:
Plan Reading & Material Takeoff

By Wayne J. DelPico

A complete course in reading and interpreting building plans—and performing quantity takeoffs to professional standards.

This book shows and explains, in clear language and with over 160 illustrations, typical working drawings encountered by contractors in residential and light commercial construction. The author describes not only how all common features are represented, but how to translate that information into a material list. Organized by CSI division, each chapter uses plans, details and tables, and a summary checklist.

$35.95 per copy
Over 420 pages, illustrated, softcover
Catalog No. 67307   ISBN 0-87629-348-8

Builder's Essentials:
Best Business Practices for Builders & Remodelers:
An Easy-to-Use Checklist System

By Thomas N. Frisby

A comprehensive guide covering all aspects of running a construction business, with more than 40 user–friendly checklists. This book provides expert guidance on: increasing your revenue and keeping more of your profit; planning for long-term growth; keeping good employees and managing subcontractors.

$29.95 per copy
Over 220 pages, softcover
Catalog No. 67329   ISBN 0-87629-619-3

Builder's Essentials:
Framing & Rough Carpentry,
2nd Edition

A complete, illustrated do-it-yourself course on framing and rough carpentry. The book covers walls, floors, stairs, windows, doors, and roofs, as well as nailing patterns and procedures. Additional sections are devoted to equipment and material handling, standards, codes, and safety requirements.

The "framer-friendly" approach includes easy-to-follow, step-by-step instructions. This practical guide will benefit both the carpenter's apprentice and the experienced carpenter, and sets a uniform standard for framing crews.

Also available in Spanish!

$24.95 per copy
Over 125 pages, illustrated, softcover
Catalog No. 67298A   ISBN 0-87629-617-7
Spanish 67298AS ISBN 0-87629-654-1

Builder's Essentials:
Advanced Framing Methods

By Scot Simpson

A highly illustrated, "framer-friendly" approach to advanced framing elements. Provides expert, but easy-to-interpret, instruction for laying out and framing complex walls, roofs, and stairs, and special requirements for earthquake and hurricane protection. Also helps bring framers up to date on the latest building code changes, and provides tips on the lead framer's role and responsibilities, how to prepare for a job, and how to get the crew started.

$24.95 per copy
250 pages, illustrated, softcover
Catalog No. 67330   ISBN 0-87629-618-5

Interior Home Improvement Costs, New 9th Edition

Estimates for the most popular remodeling and repair projects-from small, do-it-yourself jobs-to major renovations and new construction.

Includes:
- Kitchens & Baths
- New Living Space from Your Attic, Basement or Garage
- New Floors, Paint & Wallpaper
- Tearing Out or Building New Walls
- Closets, Stairs & Fireplaces
- New Energy-Saving Improvements, Home Theatres, and Much More!

$24.95 per copy
Over 250 pages, illustrated, softcover
Catalog No. 67308E   ISBN 0-87629-743-2

Exterior Home Improvement Costs, New 9th Edition

Estimates for the most popular remodeling and repair projects-from small, do-it-yourself jobs, to major renovations and new construction.

Includes:
- Curb Appeal Projects-Landscaping, Patios, Porches, Driveways and Walkways
- New Windows and Doors
- Decks, Greenhouses, and Sunrooms
- Room Additions and Garages
- Roofing, Siding, and Painting
- "Green" Improvements to Save Energy & Water

$19.95 per copy
Over 250 pages, illustrated, softcover
Catalog No. 67309E   ISBN 0-87629-742-4

Books for Builders/Annual Cost Guides

Means Illustrated Construction Dictionary, 3rd Edition

Long regarded as the Industry's finest, the *Means Illustrated Construction Dictionary* is now even better. With the addition of over 1,000 new terms and hundreds of new illustrations, it is the clear choice for the most comprehensive and current information.

The companion CD-ROM that comes with this new edition adds many extra features: larger graphics, expanded definitions, and links to both CSI MasterFormat numbers and product information.

Contains 19,000 construction words, terms, phrases, symbols, weights, measures, and equivalents. 1,000 new entries; 1,200 helpful illustrations, easy-to-use format with thumbtabs.

$99.95 per copy
Over 790 pages, illustrated, hardcover
Catalog No. 67292A   ISBN 0-87629-538-3

Historic Preservation
Project Planning & Estimating
by Swanke Hayden Connell Architects

Managing Historic Restoration, Rehabilitation, and Preservation Building Projects and Determining and Controlling Their Costs

The authors explain:
* How to determine whether a structure qualifies as historic
* Where to obtain funding and other assistance
* How to evaluate and repair more than 75 historic building materials
* How to properly research, document, and manage the project to meet code, agency, and other special requirements
* How to approach the upgrade of major building systems

$99.95 per copy
Over 675 pages, hardcover
Catalog No. 67323   ISBN 0-87629-573-1

Means Building Construction Cost Data 2005

Offers you unchallenged unit price reliability in an easy-to-use arrangement. Whether used for complete, finished estimates or for periodic checks, it supplies more cost facts better and faster than any comparable source. Over 23,000 unit prices for 2005. The City Cost Indexes now cover over 930 areas, for indexing to any project location in North America.

$115.95 per copy
Over 700 pages, softcover
Catalog No. 60015   ISBN 0-87629-750-5

Means Light Commercial Cost Data 2005

Specifically addresses the light commercial market, which is an increasingly specialized niche in the industry. Aids you, the owner/designer/contractor, in preparing all types of estimates, from budgets to detailed bids. Includes new advances in methods and materials. Assemblies section allows you to evaluate alternatives in early stages of design/planning.

$99.95 per copy
Over 650 pages, softcover
Catalog No. 60185   ISBN 0-87629-765-3

Means Residential Cost Data 2005

Speeds you through residential construction pricing with more than 100 illustrated complete house square-foot costs. Alternate assemblies cost selections are located on adjoining pages, so that you can develop tailor-made estimates in minutes. Complete data for detailed unit cost estimates is also provided.

$99.95 per copy
Over 600 pages, softcover
Catalog No. 60175   ISBN 0-87629-758-0

Means Repair & Remodeling Cost Data 2005
Commercial/Residential

You can use this valuable tool to estimate commercial and residential renovation and remodeling. By using the specialized costs in this manual, you'll find it's not necessary to force fit prices for new construction into remodeling cost planning. Provides comprehensive unit costs, building systems costs, extensive labor data and estimating assistance for every kind of building improvement.

$99.95 per copy
Over 650 pages, softcover
Catalog No. 60045   ISBN 0-87629-760-2

For more information
visit Means Web Site
at www.rsmeans.com

New Titles

Builder's Essentials: Estimating Building Costs for the Residential & Light Commercial Contractor

By Wayne J. DelPico

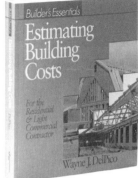

Step-by-step estimating methods for residential and light commercial contractors. Includes a detailed look at every construction specialty—explaining all the components, takeoff units, and labor needed for well-organized estimates:

Correctly interpreting plans and specifications.
Developing accurate and complete labor and material costs.
Understanding direct and indirect overhead costs.
Using historical cost data to generate new project budgets.

Plus hard-to-find, professional guidance on what to consider so you can allocate the right amount for profit and contingencies.

$29.95 per copy
Over 400 pages, illustrated, softcover
Catalog No. 67343   ISBN 0-87629-741-6

Building & Renovating Schools

This all-inclusive guide covers every step of the school construction process—from initial planning, needs assessment, and design, right through moving into the new facility. A must-have resource for anyone concerned with new school construction or renovation, including architects and engineers, contractors and project managers, facility managers, school administrators and school board members, building committees, community leaders, and anyone else who wants to ensure that the project meets the schools' needs in a cost-effective, timely manner. With square foot cost models for elementary, middle, and high school facilities and real-life case studies of recently completed school projects.

The contributors to this book – architects, construction project managers, contractors, and estimators who specialize in school construction – provide start-to-finish, expert guidance on the process.

$99.95 per copy
Over 425 pages
Catalog No. 67342   ISBN 0-87629-740-8

Means ADA Compliance Pricing Guide, New Second Edition

By Adaptive Environments and RSMeans

Completely updated and revised to the new 2004 Americans with Disabilities Act Accessible Guidelines, this book features more than 70 of the most commonly needed modifications for ADA compliance—their design requirements, suggestions, and final cost. Projects range from installing ramps and walkways, widening doorways and entryways, and installing and refitting elevators, to relocating light switches and signage, and remodeling bathrooms and kitchens. Also provided are:

Detailed cost estimates for budgeting modification projects, including estimates for each of 260 alternates.
An assembly estimate for every project, with detailed cost breakdown including materials, labor hours, and contractor's overhead.
3,000 Additional ADA compliance-related unit cost line items.
Costs that are easily adjusted to over 900 cities and towns.

Over 350 pages
$79.99 per copy
Catalog No. 67310A   ISBN 0-87629-739-4

Index